Preface

'Hypnotised By Numbers' is an advanced sports betting book with a difference. In a new world of data driven markets this book shows you how to exploit the inefficiencies and flaws in these sports betting markets across different areas and win, more old-school style. It details examples of some of my own notable bets and betting exploits down the years and the probabilistic thinking and angles behind them. We talk about applying the concept of conditional probability in probability theory which I've been using for nearly 20 years to take on the sportsbooks and poker world with a strong degree of success. HBN is the art vs science of sports betting and the art wins.

" However, there are few, who did not learn the probabilistic theory and probabilistic thinking, born to be the one who always acts on probability outcomes. For example, the master of Texas Hold'em poker or Market Wizards "

- Catherine Wang

HYPNOTISED BY NUMBERS

Psychology and logic versus data in sports and betting

By Bryan Nicholson

Introduction

The world of data is becoming more prominent in every walk of life. The betting industry has been growing increasingly data orientated over the years, exaggerated by the in-play betting boom which now accounts for over 50% of action. Modellers are taking over, and more people are learning to use algorithms and AI at the core of sports betting. Data science is a rapidly evolving field. Bettors are becoming more sophisticated, and sportsbooks have had to respond and refine their models in kind.

The same process is ongoing as the change that hit the poker world in terms of trial and error (empirical) poker experts lending their hand to building software and solvers. Up and coming players are studying these tools to learn the right moves but this is a limited exercise, as you might know the moves but not fully understand the complexities behind them - what I call: The Black Box Paradox of the betting markets.

"**Hypnotised By Numbers**" is about levelling the playing field somewhat. I show you a real way of beating the markets without needing these advanced maths or coding skills, and I convey to the reader how, and more importantly perhaps, why, this data model employed by the bookmaking and betting industry is exploitable, especially in the Highstreet. Hypnotised by numbers points out the flaws in the markets and details how to exploit these flaws. Nothing really has changed about the way I've been betting these markets for almost twenty years in terms of the angles I'm looking for. It's all about using conditional probability theory and logic to find an edge against rule of thumb mathematics. It's not viable for bookmakers to change from their model.

Understanding intrinsically how the markets work and getting to terms with the variables and dynamics of the sports you bet is key, as is being a student of probability theory and conditional probability. We need to be an expert in understanding <u>fundamental</u> sports betting maths. This book is one of, if not the first sports betting books that shows you how to both logically and mathematically beat the markets, using examples of real-life bets and conveying the thinking behind them.

"Conditional probability is the key to unlocking the betting markets"

I cover newer concepts such as strokes gained in golf and expected goals in football, and away from sports betting we also touch on solvers and game theory in poker and the permutations and combinations world of Daily Fantasy Sports.

The philosophy in my long-term methodology is now referred to as the Bayesian approach and I'm starting to see people write and hear people talk more and more about this regarding probability theory and betting. Combining this approach with watching the sports and analysing them (empirical learning) - is the way to garner a true edge vs the bookmaker.

Bayesian (Inverse p.) is the alternative probabilistic approach to what the market makers do which is a frequentist method for pricing up - a method based on the mean, median or frequency distributions that beat the average punter but have no chance against Bayesian probability sports betting sharps. That's where margins, limits and stake factoring come in for bookmaker protection.

Hypnotised By Numbers is mainly a psychology and logic-based theory (and proven) book. My third book - which is already well underway - will be mathematically based on the fundamentals that are needed for sports betting in that respect. That math required for successful winning sports betting is quite basic that anyone can be taught. I'm going to teach it to you all, right there in the one place - no rubbish you don't need to fill the pages. 2nd level education is enough to have the mathematical skills needed to potentially become a sharp player in the sports betting world.

"The feeling is I'm not the only one that has been a little irked by the new way of learning. We need more of those in the know to start talking to help protect the betting world from becoming Hypnotised By Numbers"

Table of Contents...

Author's note:

Hypnotised By Numbers is no.2 of 3 in a three-part series from Bryan Nicholson covering all areas of sports betting. The real big potential edges in betting on sports stem from a strong logic, reasoning, and problem-solving intuitive approach. I'll show you right here how psychology may just be even more important than maths in sports betting, but don't quote me on that!

Beneath the surface, sports betting is the same as poker. Not a lot of people realise this. It's all odds, probability and statistics and exploiting tendencies (market dynamics). I've been here before: what's happening in the sports betting world happened already over the last ten years in the poker world and is still ongoing. Phil Galfond, a legitimate poker elite, has spoken about the data orientated guys being set up for failure re: solvers, and I'm seeing a similar prognosis in sports betting.

Having a strong aptitude for math and numbers and mainly probability theory is necessary to beat the markets long term but there's a big difference between this and having studied advanced math in depth. That isn't needed. What you learn in secondary school math is more than enough to succeed at sports betting or poker. Anything else is largely fluff and noise if you're trying to beat the markets.

What determines the best sports bettors? It's not about how much money they bet and win. Ultimately the judge of betting skill is your long-term ROI. This equates exactly to your edge on the markets - your actual ability in spotting discrepancies in the markets and in the pricing vs the true probabilities, which is what it's ultimately all about - Understanding and uncovering flaws in universally priced algorithm-based markets. How much you stake doesn't really have a bearing on skill / ability and this is a concept people are also hypnotised by.

A Background to the Science

Winning in sports betting or finding a decent edge on the markets is about thinking probabilistically. We can use a process called empirical inference through watching the sports we bet on. The real edge vs the market lies in developing a strong intuition surrounding the sports you watch, and it's how you begin to be able to both originate odds and quantify your true price estimates - applying probability theory and psychological factors to the markets rather than the frequentist maths that they are built from. We will then have a benchmark to weigh our price estimates against.

Hypnotised by numbers points out in-depth the inefficiencies (and thus potential available exploits) in data-driven markets across the sports and the problems with fighting fire with fire using certain methods of data science. Risk intelligence and subjectivity is applied for smaller sample sizes, and we pay attention to performance in-game to help evaluate and benchmark our bets. Uncertainty can usually be quantified somewhat in sports betting. Risk intelligence is the ability to estimate probabilities accurately.

Empirical Evidence

Empirical evidence is information obtained through observation and documentation of certain behaviour and patterns or through experiment. Usually through the senses.

Many sports betting markets are built using bell curves that are called normal or gaussian distributions, and Poisson distributions, along with averages that come with their own flaws in terms of efficiency in a vacuum.

These flaws are down to lack of conditional probability factored into each market taken on its own merit. This can be beaten using a concept known as Bayesian inference which we talk about later. Several prop markets for example are flawed re distributions.

The model works for the bookmakers on average vs the regular punter and because of factoring and limiting the shrewder players. Putting all games and markets into the same population has its limits - You can't just lump everything into the same population and expect to come up with precise probabilities. Conditional probabilities are subjective and if you are smart and watch the games, you can reason well enough to compute more accurate true probabilities with practice.

Bookmaker firms haven't got the means or resources and there aren't enough people capable of pricing these markets more accurately. That's not needed overall for their model which is great for both sides of the fence. The margin is easily beatable for people who understand the exploitable flaws in the markets. Gambling is all probability theory.

What's more important than knowing where you have an edge? Knowing where you don't, or where your edge has diminished. Track your bets. Categorise them into different sports and markets...

Unlocking the markets....

Keys to winning in Sports Betting

There are several key areas to master the concept of if you want to make a good return on sports betting in the long term. The mathematical stuff can be filed under the branch of math: probability and statistics. The intuitive stuff will fall under psychology and conditional probability or logic...

Logical-mathematical intelligence

Their problem-solving ability is very striking and is often related to a type of non-verbal intelligence, i.e. they can know the answer to a certain problem long before they verbalise it.

1. There is no substitute for watching and analysing as much sport as you can to build up a strong intuition for the dynamics of the markets, nuances, variables of the sports themselves, and the odds. The more time you spend in this area and the more information and wisdom you consume the better your chances. All the best bettors are gamblers and lovers of the game itself. There's a difference in being a math expert with a strong interest in sports betting to being an expert sports bettor. How do we find an edge on the markets that others don't know of? We watch and consume information.

2. Value betting and maximising EV - expected value (or minimising your losses) is probably the most important concept in turning your betting into an investment. Expected value or EV is the mathematics of working out how much you would win or lose per bet on average if you could theoretically play the bet out under the same conditions an infinite number of times.

You can't do this, but you can play numerous bets at the same win expectation and odds with similar variables so it's much of a muchness.

Formula for expected value (EV):
(Potential Profit * probability of winning) - (stake * probability of losing)

"*Take the probability of loss times the amount of possible loss from the probability of gain times the amount of possible gain. That is what we're trying to do.*

It's imperfect, but that's what it's all about"

— Warren Buffett

Warren Buffet is well known as probably the finest investor of our time. His philosophy was all about expected value and risk management. He preferred less investments with big upside rather than a high volume of investments with smaller theoretical edge. Some of Warren's most memorable quotes are:

"Rule No. 1 never lose money. Rule No. 2 is never forget Rule No. 1"

and

"It's far better to buy a wonderful company at a fair price, than a fair company at a wonderful price"

You can see here that he's essentially putting more emphasis on minimising your losses over maximising your winnings. This brings us on to no. 3....

3. Managing and / or minimising variance and risk. The two best ways to play the market are by taking a higher volume of bets with a lower edge approach or adopting a more selective higher expected value, lesser risk, bigger staking approach, Warren Buffet style. Variance is the difference between results in the short term versus long term expectancy.

4. The Kelly Criterion or the Kelly formula is the optimal staking formula for managing sports betting EV and bank growth. Set aside a nominal bankroll amount that suits, then come up with a staking plan to allow for the law of large numbers. Make sure your betting bankroll is separate to your life roll.

5. Understanding probability theory and applying conditional probability to the markets.

This is the area of exploiting the markets. Factoring in variables / weightings to give us precise parameters that will be different to and more accurate than the frame of the markets. Unlike chance-based games that you find in a casino like roulette or craps etc, or in random number generators associated with poker and the likes where there is an actual fixed probability percentage, the actual probability in each sporting event or game is not known.

In fact, given the wide array of variables at play - which can change rapidly and significantly from game to game - the true probabilities can differ vastly from the probabilities implied by the odds. I'm not going to go too deep into the maths or expand on the four areas above here, as that will be covered in depth in book no. 3 of the modern sports betting trio. I don't want to make HBN too mathsy.

Data

Statistical modelling and advanced data science can be filed as "desirable but not essential". If you have these skills, then great but there's no substitute for watching sport and learning empirically and intuitively how to sort out the signal from small samples.

Any other more advanced maths is not necessarily needed. Running simulations and calculating p-values and stuff of that ilk is usually futile. Most people doing this will not be making money vs the sports betting markets. They will be maths experts or analytics aficionados and not betting experts, like I alluded to earlier, and there's a huge difference.

Note: There are plenty of data science boot camps out there now online should you feel the need to add data analysis to your portfolio of skills and there is no harm in doing so for life in general, never mind betting on sports.

The Bookmaker Model

Let me make it clear that the bookmakers and people that matter generally know about the overall inefficiencies in the algorithms and markets; it just doesn't matter, as their model targets the collective average and handle of all bettors and just needs to win overall. They have their limits and profiling in place as well as the margin to protect against the guys they know are smart enough to spot these inefficiencies. A decent shaped book and the ability to move the lines renders them safe overall. The fact that most of their budget now goes on advertising tells its own story.

The evolution of the bookmaker model over the last twenty years is intriguing and when I give you insight into what you are up against you might not feel so out of your depth. Many serious bettors are under an illusion in this respect.

How do the Operators set their Odds?

If you want to get ahead in the sports betting markets these days, you need to know what you're up against. The more information you have as to how the sports betting markets are formed and what drives the origination of odds and sports line movements, the better.

Data Driven Betting Odds and Markets

The sports betting industry is ever changing, and we are in a time that's becoming more and more data driven. Odds compilers, or "originators" are in shorter supply. The betting exchange has become more and more of a tool to guide market making and it now runs the show. Syndicates, select professional players / groups, consultancy companies etc seeding the markets means when they become liquid, they will be close to an accurate reflection of the fair odds for the most part. In theory anyway.

"The more money in the market, the harder it is to beat"

There's no need for sportsbooks to spend a lot of money on highly skilled odds compilers anymore. Part of the trader's brief is to make sure their prices are not bigger than the exchange to stop arbitrage betting. They can model their odds on the exchange numbers, adding in whatever margin and terms that suits them and their customer base.

The quants taking over market compilation wherever they are originating from is great news for sports bettors. There are inefficiencies everywhere and there are more sites popping up that are gathering authority and influence in their domain. This is nothing but good news for punters as it means we can be contrarian to any one establishment and then find lots of value in their mistakes and inefficiencies that have been pilfered.

Sports betting odds nowadays originate largely from consultancies, and we'll talk all about this a little further down....

The Brief of the Punter

Our number one goal in sports betting as punters or pros is finding value - making good positive expected value bets. Forget about finding your winners - what you are looking for is the biggest discrepancies you can find in the odds in terms of the price you can attain vs the true odds (to 100%) that the selection should be. The bigger this discrepancy, the more expected value you have, and therefore the more you should invest, theoretically. We also need to factor in risk.

We talked about the Kelly formula above. When your predicted expected value is increasing you should stake more (in proportion) on these selections to maximise the value in the price. This is how you win long term in betting without relying on luck. It's the *only way* you can win long term without variance just being in your favour over your betting lifespan.

You need to know how your opposition operates if you are going to beat them. This is a general rule, not just for sports betting. A common misconception is that you are dealing with some sort of sports betting geniuses in the trading rooms and bookie headquarters. You're not. In fact, many of the "experts" in this area of compiling accurate odds have moved on or are sitting at home in their underpants like me.

Maybe they've taken up new roles in B2B odds consultancies or betting syndicates, decided to have a go at becoming a full-time professional bettor, or even moved on altogether to a different sector. The betting positions encompass the guys who really control the betting markets. Traders in your high street bookie HQs are now for the most part middlemen.

What would you say if I told you that if you were looking to apply to be a trader at one of these big firms now that on-the-job specs it might say that you don't even need expert or even good knowledge of the sports betting domain? What you need is a college degree in some form of mathematics.

"Sports betting knowledge desirable but not essential"

Where do the betting odds originate from?

There are some originators at the bigger companies or sharp bookmakers like Pinnacle, BetCris or Circa Sports (American books). Most UK and Ireland / European betting outlets are supplied by B2B odds and sports betting or data consultancy companies now. The odds, lines and data for the sports betting markets are outsourced to the likes of Kambi, Abelson Info, Entain and BetRadar etc.

These guys will be copied by a lot of the softer books. The big Asian betting companies or sharp books like Pinnacle control the odds and lines in the football markets and expected goals (xG) are now incorporated into odds in specific football matches when they are being compiled. They are used by the big syndicates like Star Lizard and SmartOdds.

Beating the bookmaker Margin - the Overround or Vigorish

The margins (or overround) is how the sportsbooks make their money. This is called the "hold" in the US market. The overround or combined margin is the percentage the bookmakers add to their books that give them their vigorish/juice (commission) advantage.

In a perfect world the sum of all selection's implied probabilities in the market books will add up to 100% when the originators price up: Of course, this isn't the case - they will add to more than this when you sum all the implied probabilities from the all the possible outcomes together, given the small percentage margin added to the individual selections.

The lines will move from the weight of money from the sports betting handicappers (who independently price to 100%) or the public recreational bettors or hobbyists. At the sharp books - some of the bigger players control the lines which filter through the industry. Reverse line movement can occur when some sharp players place money down against the weight of public money.

The aim is usually to balance the book thus trying to secure profit no matter the result of the game, but that's a rare feat. The overround is what protects the bookmaker, and commission (vigorish) is calculated using the formula overleaf...

Overround (hold) Formula for calculating Juice / Vigorish

If two teams on the moneyline or the NFL spreads are priced up 10/11 vs 10/11 (-110 vs -110 American odds), to get the implied percentage of the odds, first off, we divide the denominator by the (numerator + denominator) then multiply by 100 which would be:

1. $(11/21 = 0.5238) \times 100 = 52.4\%$ (rounded off)
2. Do the same for the other side and as you can see 52.4+52.4 does not add to 100%, it adds to 104.8%. This 4.8% is the book overround (total margin) or the "hold".
3. To calculate the commission percentage which is the juice/vigorish, use the formula:

Vig Formula: 1 - (1/book %) x 100, then turn it into a percentage.

IE: 1- (1/104.8) * 100 = 0.0458.

Multiply x 100 to turn it into a percentage of 4.58% which is the bookmaker cut, written as a percentage of total turnover (turnover is the "handle" in US terminology). As you can see the overround margin (or hold in US) isn't quite the same as the commission (juice / vigorish) in terms of being written as a percentage figure on handle.

How do Bookies win?

There are two different types of sportsbooks - the sharp book model and the recreational book model.

- Sharp
- Recreational

The sharp book model

This model consists of three departments:

1. Risk
2. Data Scientists (Bayesian, with sports knowledge),
3. Quants

That's the optimal blend. That's the Pinnacle model - straight from trading director Marco Blume's mouth. I'd advocate for you to spend a lot of time studying how the markets work and what pricing them up involves - this is how a true edge in sports betting can be garnered.

"To beat the markets, you must fully understand the markets"

The sharp book model is a proper bookmaking model - one you'd look to emulate if running an independent bookmaker service, albeit maybe not to such high limits. Pinnacle is a sharp book which offers high limits and low margins.

The limits are higher for more popular sports and more mature markets. Marco Blume calls his biggest sharp players his betting consultants who hammer his lines into place. They use Bayesian style models, they have a blend of quants, domain knowledge and risk experts.

The Highstreet Bookmaker

The recreational sportsbook does not work this way. Rec or "soft" books have bigger margins for profit and protection, their prices are based on universal algorithms using big data averages, copying exchanges and other books, and have odds imported from b2b companies. This is the general approach albeit there will be some individual operator nuance and some guys in house that still price up. Essentially these Highstreet firms like Coral or PaddyPower or William Hill are a marketing firm with much of their budget going on advertising. They will stake factor and limit sharp players who can beat or look like they have the necessary skills or domain knowledge to beat them. Beating the odds in these bookmakers by being selective and line shopping is the easy part.

There are still many highly skilled and knowledgeable sports bettors and traders working in house in the soft books, especially when we start looking towards the heads of departments. I personally know some top dogs still in these positions. These guys sometimes like to take on various odds they are responsible for that the market is dictating. What I mean by that is the odds don't necessarily reflect their opinion and they might have a bet on the event elsewhere. If you monitor the odds fluctuations in the markets over the course of a few weeks, you can start to see how fickle these sports betting markets are - the way the odds ebb and flow in such a short space of time based on recent form and results. It doesn't make a whole lot of sense at all when you follow it and think about it.

For example: How can a golfer be 33/1 one week then 80/1 three weeks later in the same field?

The reality is that every player or team has a true baseline price. Yet, the odds most weeks will be either below or above this threshold, often significantly. Our objective then as bettors is to spot the trends and patterns which tell us when these selections are likely to both outperform and underperform the baseline and manipulate these odds in our favour. It's quite simple when you break it down that way, but you need to put in a lot of time watching the sports to be able to do this. If you're just using models, you will have a hard time identifying the patterns in the data - the signal from the noise. The ability to estimate or know true prices is only half the battle, no matter what way you derive these fair odds:

- Models
- Smarts
- Steam chasing
- Piggy backing
- Reputable tipsters
- Empirically
- Logical lateral thinking
- Rankings

The Signal and the Noise

The *Signal And The Noise* is a book written by Nate Silver and the theme is basically about finding true patterns buried in the data science world, largely using conditional probability theory (Bayesian inference). I talk later on in the book about the **clustering illusion** and how that's not that relevant in sports betting.

One of the more baffling chapters of my gambling experience looking at social media came via an emerging trend of the winner of a particular golf tournament. It was at Torrey Pines where half the field tees it up on each of two individual courses over the first couple of days. In eight tournaments in a row the winner had started on the tougher South Course at Torrey and golf gambling twitter were convinced there was something predictive in it when in fact it was completely random.

Why?

Because there was no logical explanation or reason behind it. This trend was put to bed with the sequence going from eight-in-a-row to three-in-a row the other way and that's the last we heard of it. The latest winner was Luke List who started back on the South again.

But what if there had been a potential logical reason behind this trend?

Let's say for example that the top thirty seeded players in the event were mandatory starters at the south course on day one. How would this change the probability from 50/50 (winner from either course on day one)? **Bayes Theorem** comes into play here.

We can deduce using some qualitative analysis:

First, we could look at the odds from upcoming golf tournaments and see where the prices lie 30 deep in the market. This is usually around the 66 to 80/1 mark in a full field event.

Now we can look at some historical big data and see how many tournament winners went off at 66/1 or less. If we found from a decent sample that 70% of tournaments are won by one of the top thirty golfers in the field we can then infer that the South course is 70% likely vs 30% to produce the winner having teed it up there on day one. In reality it's 50/50.

To put this in a betting context, let's say you knew the top thirty were going to tee it up at one course and the bookmakers didn't and they offered a market on "which side of the draw will the winner come from" at 10/11 a piece (margin incorporated) in a pick'em. 10/11 (1.91 or -110) represents a 52.4% chance and bookmaker juice is included in the price.

Your break even percentage on a 70% chance is 1.43 which is around 4/9 in fractional odds. Backing the 10/11 would represent around 33.7% Expected Value (EV) in this situation. Several opportunities like this arise in all sorts of betting markets and sports markets throughout the year and they are often repeatable.

This is a lesson on finding the true signal in a small sample of data and if you can get your head around it the sky's the limit in sports betting. If there is an actual logical reason or variable behind a trend emerging in small data, you'd be silly to poo poo it in sports betting - this is your hidden magic potion.

The Art of Sports Betting.... let's tuck in

Betting On the Olympics

Why am I starting with the Olympics? It's not random. I want to bring a concept strongly to your attention: the more obscure markets are where the real edges lie.

Here we have **Akani Simbine** on the Oddschecker grid. He had recently set the men's African 100 metre sprint record at 9.84 seconds, and bear in mind Usain Bolt's record was 9.58 seconds. As you can see, he's third favourite but he ranges in odds from 10/3 to 10/1 across the books. In my experience, obscure markets or these kinds of Olympic type markets are ambiguous and often we can play one book off against another in various scenarios and submarkets to get value on what is generally a true price somewhere in the middle.

Marcel Jacobs was the eventual winner of that 100m event at a whopping 33/1 top price heading into the Athletics. The point of this is that the lack of appropriate data will always leave odds open to interpretation, and thus opportunities, and the more obscure the event the better. This is the main event of the Athletics just before the off and apparently no one in the odds compiling or trading offices knew of Jacobs potential or form. There was not enough "data" to price the market correctly.

Swimming Against the Tide

In the Olympics Swimming we had **Lydia Jacoby** to win the 100m Breaststroke priced at around 30 to 1 pre-final. She had come into the event at 7/2 and had drifted all the way out due to her times in the qualifiers. These times can be deceptive as athletes generally are not giving it their all in the heats or the semis. Without efficient data to go on the odds compilers will have difficulty assessing the correct prices. Jacoby went on to win and was only seventeen years of age at the time.

We saw a similar result in the freestyle with **Siobhan Haughey**. Siobhan was 2nd to **Ariarne Titmus** in the women's 200m Freestyle and Titmus talked in an interview about knowing how much Haughey "wanted it", after they contested the 400m final and the Aussie won. Siobhan was still available as high as 20 to 1 to win gold in the upcoming 100m freestyle.

The books were not too quick to move prices in events that were related to other key events. The 20s and high prices lasted for a decent amount of time and then when Siobhan had qualified for the final of the 100m with ease she had been cut to 4s across the board, now 2nd fave behind much fancied **Emma McKeon**, another Aussie.

The Aussie swimmer McKeon ended up beating Haughey in the final by the slimmest of margins of 0.31 seconds. This shows how we can find opportunities, ew bets, and of course more serious players will have had plenty of chances to hedge or trade their bets on Haughey. I don't recall if and what the EW terms were but I'm sure there was a decent opportunity there as well going by other markets.

No Hurdles for the Femke Fatale

Dutch women's hurdles boss **Femke Bol** was a rising star ahead of Japan 2021, but she had at least one if not two other world class girls to beat if she was going to get her hands on the gold medal in the 400m Hurdles. This final was going to be serious with three world-class women pushing each other all the way. We had seen the world record broken in the men's 400m hurdles the night previous by **Karsten Warholm**.

Note: these bets were discussed by me on twitter one and two days in advance and there was ample time and opportunity to get on.

The odds in the below images are for the women's world record in the 400m hurdles to be broken. There was a bit of time and a few quid matched at 2.14 and above on Betfair exchange when money came into the market. Liquidity got plenty higher than what we see and prices such as Skybets were readily available. Scroll down and see the Skybet price in the sportsbook.

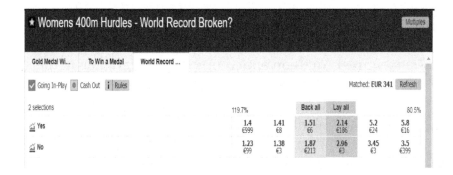

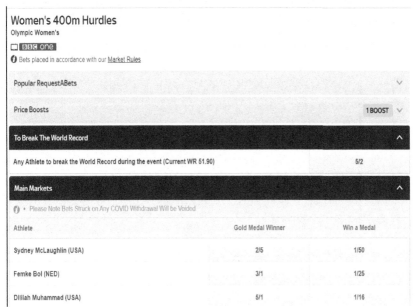

Women's 400m Hurdles
Olympic Women's

☐ BBC one

ℹ Bets placed in accordance with our Market Rules

Popular RequestABets	∨

Price Boosts	1 BOOST ∨

To Break The World Record	∧
Any Athlete to break the World Record during the event (Current WR 51.90)	5/2

Main Markets		∧

ℹ • Please Note Bets Struck on Any COVID Withdrawal Will be Voided

Athlete	Gold Medal Winner	Win a Medal
Sydney McLaughlin (USA)	2/5	1/50
Femke Bol (NED)	3/1	1/25
Dililah Muhammad (USA)	5/1	1/16

Skybet price boost on the world record to be beaten was way off base

The pundits were talking about a "fast track" and new running gear the athletes had access to that year in Japan and these variables were taking time off their runs. We saw a similar scenario in the women's 400m straight run when **Femke Bol** ran her heat in a very strong time and contracted from 5s to 3s. She then was drafted in to run the 4x400m relay for the Dutch team and started to drift a little again for the hurdles and bet365 pushed her all the way out to 6s. This was a mistake. Bol won her 400m hurdle semi-final at a canter and came back into 3s on the machine.

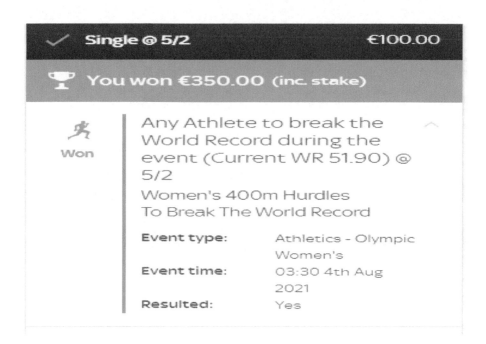

Single @ 5/2   €100.00

🏆 You won €350.00 (inc. stake)

🏃 Won

Any Athlete to break the
World Record during the
event (Current WR 51.90) @
5/2
Women's 400m Hurdles
To Break The World Record

Event type:	Athletics - Olympic Women's
Event time:	03:30 4th Aug 2021
Resulted:	Yes

The key variable here as mentioned above was that the track was being talked about as a faster track while the runners the athletes were wearing supposedly helped them run a small bit quicker. If you were following the coverage you'd have heard about these narratives. Narratives usually have traction for a reason. We'd already seen the men smash the record with Karsten Warholm, and two guys beat it in the final.

The top two in this women's 400m hurdles final ended up beating the world record while Femke Bol also set a new European record. There were OK Limits at the likes of SkyBet. Overall, we were seeing faster times. These factors play such a huge part in finding an edge in sports betting and are usually underestimated by the market and more so the odds compilers. It's conditional probability that trumps baseline frequentist probabilities. It's not like cards or roulette when the odds are the odds. Narratives can be vital. We are looking for angles that are not priced into the odds and quite often there will be narratives that are very significant and demand a serious re draft if accurate odds are required.

The fact is this market had three superstars as the top three in the betting, and the world record was under big threat. There was an arb available for quite a few hours backing Sky Bet's 5/2 (decent liquidity / limits) then laying around the 2.0 mark on Betfair. Skybet then cut it to even money later in the day before the final.

We will see later on with subjective factors and "narratives" including course fit in golf, and how it's not taken into consideration nearly as much as it should be still in this day and age. Variables such as weather as well are so key in several sports, mainly golf.

The point of all this is to show how and why odds compiled predominantly by data and algorithms can be exploited with a bit of work and research. There's only so much that can be done in obscure markets in terms of pricing. Odds are often not as efficient as the masses are led to believe and it's the same across all sports, using the same theory and logic to beat them.

Bryan Nicholson @NicsPicks · Aug 2

This is the women's 400m hurdles market. Femke Bol eased through here heat. She's high profile. 3s - 6s available. Bet 365 pushed her out after she was drafted in to run in 4x400 relay for Dutch. Plenty of recovery time. Should go close on times

♡ 1   ↻ 1   ♡ 3   ↑   ᴵₗₗ

Bryan Nicholson @NicsPicks · Aug 2

just eased thru here semi and tightening on the machine. Interesting

Herr-ah Elaine

There was another great example of the unknown when **Elaine Thompson Herrah** was available at around 7s for the 100 metres in Japan after running close to the world record in a high-profile event just a few weeks prior. You can see the downward trend in Elaine Thompson's price with money coming in for her in the 200 metres. You might not realise that a lot of the prices at the bigger end were available for a time after she blitzed the 100m final. These events are hugely correlated, and traders should have been on the ball cutting straight away after the 200m but it didn't happen, it was far from immediate.

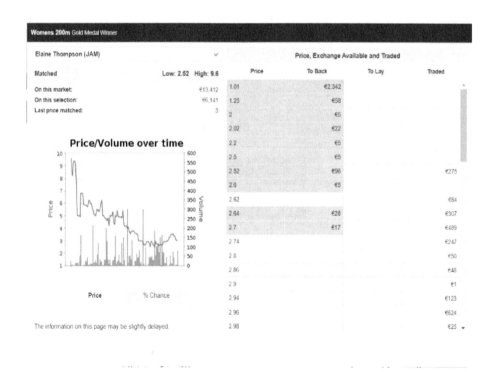

Selections: Elaine Thompson — Today / All History   Odds Shortening ☐   Odds Drifting

Time	bet365	sky bet	PADDYPOWER	William HILL	888sport	betfair	BETVICTOR	UNIBET	BET	BETFRED	SBK	betway	BoyleSports	10	SPORT NATION	novibet	VBET	SPORTING INDEX	GENTING BET	REDZONE	SPREAD EX
2021-08-01	11/8	6/4				6/4				5/4 11/8			6/4								
2021-07-31	6/4 5	7/5 7/2	6/4		7/5 7/2	7/2	6/4 9/2	6/4 7/4	6/4 4				7/4 9/4 5/2 7/2 4	6/4 7/4	6/4 7/4			7/5 9/2		6/4 7/4	
2021-07-30	11/2		13/2			13/2 11/2	13/2 15/2	4	6				11/2 6	4	4			13/2		4	

Mon Mome and the Grand National Win

If a horse tires when running up a hill once, is a sample size of one enough? Arguably. Do we need 1000 iterations to know for certain that the horse can't stay, or can we take away those three zeros and know for sure just by watching that one race? I'd argue we can - so long as nothing out of the ordinary has happened. For example, the horse had been hit with food poisoning. In other words, if the variables theoretically stayed the same there's no reason to suggest that this horse would ever fare differently if the race was repeated. That hill at Cheltenham won't get flatter.

My strategy and thinking behind Mon Mome's big moment at the winning of the Grand National was to research horses that could stay the three-mile stretch, and then back high odds on the exchange in anticipation of fall variance.

At the time, half the horses were expected to fall in the National. It was obviously random as to which ones - the faves no more likely to go the distance than the dogs.

I did my study and found five horses that fit my criteria. All were three figs on the exchange. **Mon Mome** was one of them at 100/1 with the books and 200.0 on Betfair. I only had a few quid on it as it was just a fun bet for me. As anticipated though a high number of horses fell in the National that year, and luckily Mon Mome stayed the pace and stormed home to victory.

Now I know little or nothing about specific horses and racing betting is not my forte, but all markets work the same and you just need to understand how different variables come into play. There's no substitute for watching when it comes to this. That goes for all sports and markets.

In the horse racing industry, a lot of the early action has been toned down. We have 'best odds guaranteed' (BOG). Overnight odds are often just put-up willy nilly with little effort, keeping limits very low. Backing these prices, I know can be frowned upon nowadays by traders especially, not to mention causing problems with your account. A lot of the action now comes very close to the off, especially on the exchange. The closing line in popular races will usually be much more efficient than in a lot of other sports. The Betfair starting price (BSP) is usually considered an efficient line on average in racing.

Best Odds Guaranteed (BOG) is a brilliant horse racing concession where you can take an early price about a particular horse and know that you'll either get paid out at these odds or the starting price depending on which one is bigger

I often refer to horse racing being very similar to golf betting when it comes to researching and handicapping to find an edge, but it also has some big advantages.

1. The ability to specialise
2. Do your work and knock off
3. The odds range you are working with is the perfect target

The best horse racing bettors and handicappers will be avid studiers of the specific tracks and how each horse stands up to the test - whether it be soft or firm, long or short, hilly, or flat. All horses will react differently in different conditions, and this is where a big edge can come from.

Racing bettors can profile the form, the jockeys, and the horses themselves. It's the same for golf tournaments where it's like one massive horse race, extended over four days. With racing if you specialise in a particular type of race you can focus on this. You can research the night before and then bet and just watch the races the next day and switch off at dinner time.

If you are more of a favourite backer, you can target races that suit. If you like to pick off each way value, you can target 12+ runner races and shop around for lines and even bet at books offering extra place terms. The best thing about either method though is that it is low variance. Get a decent volume of bets in over a given month and your returns should usually be somewhere close to expected if you've handicapped well. These odds ranges are also quite exploitable and there's often plenty of value on the table.

As I alluded to earlier, if you are putting your bets on the night before in racing it's frowned upon somewhat by the traders and industry insiders but that's part and parcel of the game, especially nowadays. What pro is going to wait for more efficient lines to get bets down, providing he is happy with the earlier limits? Knowing where you *don't* have an edge is something pros excel in.

What is really happening here is there's a bit of 'how dare you exploit my crappy prices' going on by the in-housers. I mentioned that there won't be a lot of effort going into the opening show of prices on certain races, especially if put up the previous night, or with firms who do some of their own odds originating. For professionals nowadays the game has changed somewhat. Taking early prices at lower limits knowing restrictions are coming is part and parcel. This will generally happen even if you're not being shrewd so losing accounts is part of the game. It's the other side of the fence that are the unfair ones restricting you for exploiting what is their shoddy work. Networking and having lots of outs and accounts is a big part of it going forward as I talk about later in Hypnotised By Numbers.

In golf for example, we can do some things to make betting it less of a grind and to narrow the playing field to make it more like the racing - lower variance, a bigger strike rate, and more rest. Don't underestimate that last word.

- Betting in play - 1st, 2nd, 3rd round leader markets
- Play the submarkets
- Bet the top nationalities
- Trade between the rounds

Some bettors don't even get involved until the weekend when a golf tournament really does play like an extended horse race.

What is A/E (actual / expected) in Horse Racing Betting?

Like the concepts behind CLV or EV/ ROI in other sports and betting, Actual Over Expected (A/E) is a way for horse bettors to track performance and potential value. In this process we multiply the probability of winning (implied by the odds or SP) for each race the horse ran in, then divide the number of actual wins by this number. So if a horse went off at 2/1 (or 3.0 or +200) five times and won two of them, the maths would be: $2/(5*0.33) = 1.2$ (If we have different race probabilities we sum them all together). Therefore, the A/E is 1.2. Anything over 1 means the horse is running better than expected according to the odds and has therefore been providing value, and vice versa. You'll obviously need to weigh up the horse's price in the next race though.

There are many variables to consider when weighing up a horse's chances. From times, jockey, ground, trainer, weights, track type and a myriad of other factors to find angles. Maybe you don't know a lot about the racing yourself and this is where the "Judge of Judges" concept comes in. The markets work the same as any other sport. If I'm going to a big meeting such as Leopardstown or Punchestown I'll take the opinion of three or four horse racing guys I respect and try to find crossovers. Then I'll monitor the market moves the night before and, on the day, and see if I can find value according to the "Judges" opinion. I've had several successful outings doing this without knowing much about the horse racing nuance itself.

Rugby World Cup Bet

An example of one of the worst bets I've ever made comes from the Rugby World Cup in 2019. This is also probably a good example of why you should be careful attacking sports you don't fully understand. You can learn more from making bad bets than you can making good bets so it's important for me to write a few of these in the book.

For me this was a large enough bet too. The theory behind it was taking advantage of an offer from a certain bookmaker who were paying out seven places each way in the top try scorer market. With my lack of knowledge of Rugby itself, after doing some research and crunching some numbers I concluded that three tries would be enough for a full place in this market. A little maths later I had targeted two players with stakes proportioned so that if just one of them scored (at least) three tries I'd be freerolling for the 'W' or two each way place returns. The two players I wanted onside were Sevu Reece of New Zealand and Jacob Stockdale of Ireland.

Long story short: they managed a woeful two tries between them. What's more, as you can see from the table below, is that three tries for either would have been useless anyway. I had failed to consider many variables such as the humidity over in Japan which might explain Stockdale's non-existence in that tournament.

When thinking Sevu Reece would be flying in the tries for New Zealand, I didn't consider squad rotation. The All Blacks even had one of their games cancelled due to a typhoon to add to the disaster…

Top try scorers

Rank	Player	Position	Tries scored
1	Josh Adams (Wales)	Wing	7
2	Makazole Mapimpi (South Africa)	Wing	6
3	Kotaro Matsushima (Japan)	Wing	5
4	Ben Smith (New Zealand)	Wing	4
5	Julian Montoya (Argentina)	Hooker	4
6	Kenki Fukuoka (Japan)	Wing	4
7	Andrew Conway (Ireland)	Wing	3
8	Beauden Barrett (New Zealand)	Full-back	3
9	Cobus Reinach (South Africa)	Scrum-half	3
10	Dane Haylett-Petty (Australia)	Wing	3
11	George Horne (Scotland)	Scrum-half	3

12	Luke Cowan-Dickie (England)	Hooker	3
13	Mbongeni Mbonambi (South Africa)	Hooker	3
14	Telusa Veainu (Tonga)	Full-back	3
15	Jonny May (England)	Wing	3
16	Marika Koroibete (Australia)	Wing	3
17	Jordie Barrett (New Zealand)	Utility back	3
18	Manu Tuilagi (England)	Centre	3
19	Cheslin Kolbe (South Africa)	Wing	3

As you can see, I was a whole try off with my estimates, and this is a great example of the limitations of using bare data without domain knowledge and experience in the nuance of the individual sport you are betting.

Football Fever and Expected Goals

We'll get stuck into some football betting and angles we can exploit on the pitch but first a little story about covid, massive variable changes in the sports, and how they affect the market probabilities...

The 2021 season during the Covid period was a real eye opener and put some thoughts and concepts about sports betting into perspective. Everything changed - from the sports to the variables to the markets. If you'd ever wondered just how much psychology affected the sports, the markets, and the true probabilities, this was prime time to see it and indeed try to expose it. We could see straight away that the football matches were all flat. **Intensity and action dropped** all over the pitch and the sportsbooks were in their element. We saw some crazy stuff.

Brighton away to Burnley were priced at evens and it was the same for Arsenal away to Everton when Everton were flying under Ancelotti and Arsenal were struggling in the early Arteta days. It turns out the prices were influenced largely by 'expected goals' (xG).

Betting

We employ the best and most respected betting brains in the industry to distil what's happening on and off the pitch, and convert it into betting probabilities.

If Totals and win-draw-win prices are going to be set using expected goals, there are many flaws in this concept so it will be very open to exploitation, just like in those games. Prices looked so random without fans, and home advantage was out the window which any savvy punter could have told you it would be at the start of Covid. Looking deeper into it, Brighton had been on a run of away wins which meant sweet nothing in the grand scheme of things.

In the Covid hit 2021 season home wins were down 10% across the top five leagues in Europe. In the English Premier League there were more away wins than home wins for the first time ever with over ten games in the difference of wins.

Expected Goals (xG)

There are a lot of flaws in the expected goals concept, and I fully expect the models to become a lot more efficient and sophisticated as time goes by. The big football betting syndicates will be using more sophisticated xG models as I write.

I had a theory a long time ago when I was a regular punter in the over +2.5 goals market that Monday night football produced more goals and action. It was more empirically observed and documented, and without loads of data I just felt like these games were great to bet the overs if the price was around evens or better.

I had a hunch that it was to do with the atmosphere, often under the lights at the 8pm kick-off time slot when plenty of the fans had those after work beers down them. I used to love betting at grounds like White Heart Land and Upton Park - tight, compact grounds with smaller pitches. I felt like players were more up for evening kick-offs back then. At the time a lot of the more flamboyant teams did tend to feature on the Monday night football, and it seemed like it never disappointed.

The covid period brought all this back to me in a period of longing and nostalgia for football of old, and after the resumption of normal football with the fans back in the stadium it was like footy was back with a vengeance. There were 34 goals scored that weekend, and the xG was off the scales. This opening weekend of the Premier League post Covid saw 34 goals scored from 28.41(xG). Shots, action, and cards unsurprisingly fell way down during the covid hit season as motivation and intensity dropped off the charts.

"We'd won nine titles in a row, and some players just got to the end of the road. You could see it pre-season, the body language, they weren't with us. You could smell it. Some players could have played and didn't, i wouldn't say, feigning injury. That eats into the dressing room." You got great pros being dragged down by guys who don't want to be there. Before lockdown we'd been rampant but after three months the environment changes, players found it difficult to adjust"

- *Neil Lennon on the mood at Celtic during the no fans Covid hit period*

Back in the day we saw the 4-4-2 formation as commonplace and there were plenty of strikers on board. Nowadays midfields are more crowded which is terrible for goals. We need loose central midfields for high scoring games, even more so than loose defences.

Harry Kane has outperformed his xG in each of the last six Premier League seasons.

20/21: 23 goals (21.10 xG)
19/20: 18 (12.99)
18/19: 17 (15.60)
17/18: 30 (26.46)
16/17: 29 (18.74)
15/16: 25 (22.73)

Coincidence or evidence towards what's wrong with expected goals concept and model?

Just like many bookmaker models and algorithms based on averages from the data, the outputs will be inefficient and therefore open to exploitation. Harry Kane has outperformed his expected goals (xG) because he is a better finisher than the average player against whom the expectancy stats are based. Expected goals does not factor in blocked shots or strong positions created that don't end in a shot being taken either. xG is a measure of the average ability (there's that word again). Anything based on the average in betting can be exploited.

If we have a Mo Salah in this position his finishing rate will be way higher than the average, so the figures don't tell the truth. There are numerous xG models all coming up with different figures and they all depend on the specific variables used and the weights plugged into them.

Let's look at how the expected goals model is affecting style of play on the field....

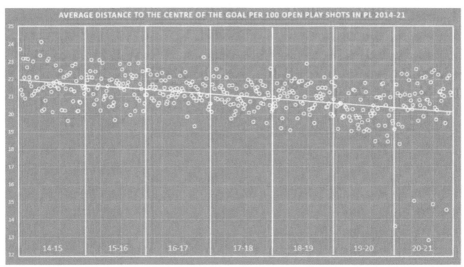

Plot of a shot graph that Pinnacle's Mark Taylor posted to Twitter

"The continuing influence of xG on declining open play shooting distances since 2014-15, although with crowds largely absent last season there were batches of games where teams went slightly rogue" - Mark Taylor

What is all this about?

Data started creeping into football probably before many of us realised. It's changing the way the game is played. Teams are now being coached to create the "better" chance and get closer to the goal before shooting. Long shots are becoming frowned upon more, hence the declining shot distances in the plot above. Short corners are the latest trend to emerge. They were always a thing but now there is even more emphasis on working the perfect position before crossing the ball.

We must be careful with all these new trends when betting as they are a *real* reason why we might see a drawdown in our results. When the variables change in sports we are betting on, we must adapt and therefore it's so important to record and document all our results - to be able to spot changes in gameplay and betting trends, and therefore results, quickly and efficiently.

Sabermetrics and Moneyball

Matthew Benham, who owns Brentford FC and the betting consultancy SmartOdds was using the sabermetrics approach to find cheap players to bring Brentford up the leagues. He did the same with his Danish team FC Midtjylland. You may remember *Football Manager*. I loved this type of thing and my claim to fame was bringing Westham from the 1st division to beating Barcelona in the final of the champions league. Sabermetrics is pretty like the strategy or concept involved there and it wouldn't surprise me at all if a young Matthew Benham got his ideas from playing this game!

In Moneyball a young data scientist weighs up all the metrics in Baseball and is working for one of the top MLB teams. He catches the attention of Brad Pitt's character (manager of a lesser team on a small budget) and is recruited by him. It's remarkably like what I've been doing with course fit in golf since before the era of the Strokes Gained metrics. This data scientist in the film is super smart and knows how to sort the signal from the noise in the data - he doesn't just run numbers and simulations. It then allows him to target lesser fancied players that maybe have some flaws that he can get on the cheap. It's a good analogy with betting high odds players in golf that are not fancied by the market in certain weeks but should be. It's the same kind of concept behind my course fit profiling manual and model. Moneyball is a good easy watch and I recommend you fire it up on Netflix if this is your sort of thing.

Sam Allardyce was one of the first I remember to bring the data analysis into his own team room in the English Premier League. He used to do all sorts with the Bolton team. Big Sam ran data analysis on his players post-match and in game to try and get any sort of extra edge he could. All the other clubs have since followed suit and it's a big part of today's game.

Dustin Johnson and Bryson were two of the first players I heard about using the likes of trackman religiously in golf. Bryson took it on a level and targets tracks where he has good course fit. Imagine what you can do in betting if you have the combination of empirical genius and predictive analysis skills - a qualitative and quantitative expert. Bill Benter or Billy Walters? Bill Benter is the perfect example of a sports betting genius. He beat the markets for millions using a quantitative and qualitative approach with his model incorporating several subjective variables which he weighted extremely efficiently.

Being able to do this and combining what I call smart betting or outside the box thinking with the data, is the optimal approach. The limitation with models is that most are based on efficient but not precise info. The real accurate price can only come from informed subjective analysis via guys with extremely high betting IQ like Benter.

Key variables to beat the goal index markets in football

What do we need to know about overs and totals betting in football (soccer)? Having studied the overs betting in the past, a few variables you should look for are:

1. Loose Defence

Are any key defensive players injured? Do the fullbacks attack? Disorganised set ups and teams who place emphasis on attacking are all factors that lead to gaps at the back.

1. Three or four top strikers on show in the game

An open game is not enough; the over 2.5 goals will not be hit enough times to overcome the odds long term if there are not enough top-quality finishers to put away the chances. This is a very significant point and a concept I learned the hard way. Nowadays with usually just one out and out striker on show, the edges are not as much in betting overs vs the prices on offer.

1. Pace in attack

For plenty of clear-cut chances/ one on ones in a game, pace in behind is key. Pace on the wings and in attack also stretches the game and opens it up. When two attacking teams meet, this is why we see fireworks.

1. Only one defensive midfielder

There's nothing worse to stifle a game than two teams playing with two or even three defensive central midfielders. With the likes of Klopp and Guardiola now making teams focus on more possession-based attacking football, it is better for the over 2.5 goals backers. This is probably the most overlooked factor and the first thing I look for - How many defensive Makelele or Kante or Fabinho type players are flooding the midfield?

Michael Owen - Wolfsburg vs Man Utd

One of my best bets I can remember making was one I shared in a blog preview of the Wolfsburg vs Man Utd match in the Champions League December 2009. An injury hit Man UTD needed a win to top the group. At the time I was following Wolfsburg a bit as they were one of the most attacking teams around with the likes of Grafite and Dzeko up front, and Hasebe and Misimovic in behind. Josue was probably their only holding player and the full backs bombed forward as well, leaving all sorts of gaps at the back. They basically hit all the overs criteria above.

Having been a Liverpool fan I knew all about a certain Michael Owen's game - playing on the shoulder of the last line of defence and using his pace to get in behind. I knew Man Utd were injury ravaged and I had heard Owen was set to start despite not playing too much football at the time. Now this opens up a great opportunity to exploit the data based footy markets.

UTD already had qualification secured but needed the win to top the group. In my mind's eye I saw this combination of the loose Wolfsburg side pushing forward leaving huge spaces for Michael Owen to exploit. Aware of Owen's finishing prowess and style of play I waded in on the anytime goal scorer market, the 'to score a brace' market, and it was also one of the only times I ever ventured into the 'to score a hattrick' market. The prices were 3/1, 20/1 and 100/1 respectively.

These odds were derived from data showing Owen's recent minutes and goals ratio. Nothing like the variables above I described is ever factored into these markets / prices, as that would be subjective opinion. Opinion doesn't have much of a part to play in the trading rooms these days.

Michael Owen duly obliged, scoring three goals, but the most satisfying thing about the bets was the way the game panned out - exactly as I projected. Wolfsburg pushed forward and they were wider than a wizard's sleeve at the back. Owen got a handful of 1-on-1s in behind in this game with Man UTD picking off Wolfsburg on the counter attack with slide rule passes and Mchael playing on the shoulder. Owen could have had five goals.

James Rodriguez top scorer World Cup 2014

This was one of my finest bets that I shared in the football back in the day and one plenty of people on the blog took advantage of. I still get people referencing it when the big tourney footy comes around! This one is more a case of fastest finger first and how we can use platforms like Twitter to take advantage of quick information filtering through.

At the time, James Rodriguez (Hammez!) and Radamel Falcao were playing for Monaco, and they were Colombia's two best players and leading hopes going into the World Cup. Colombia were a strong team at the time and much fancied underdogs. Unfortunately for Falcao he picked up an injury and info filtered through that he was not going to feature at the World Cup. I knew a bit about Rodriguez and his finishing ability, and rumour through the grapevine was that he'd now be playing a much more central role in the absence of the top striker. Fancying Colombia as I did to go deep in the tournament, I searched around for best quotes on 'James' and there was 200s EW top scorer available in a few sportsbooks.

Colombia looked great but came up against host nation Brazil in the quarter finals and were dumped out. Fortunately, James Rodriguez scored a consolation penalty in the 80th minute to bag his 6th goal of the tournament and win the golden boot. It was one of my bigger wins and finest bets. All the sweeter that several others benefited from it too. Above is an example of how information about different variables and factors themselves are the key to unlocking the markets. In the same World Cup in a hot climate and with a different ball being used that was better aerodynamically, the narrative was around players being encouraged to shoot. This was opposed to slow intensity play and players passing around the back and being told not to shoot with expected goals theory, like is happening nowadays in the top leagues. The result of this was a mountain of superb longshot goals and anyone playing in the 'to score outside box' market was being treated to some very tastily priced winners throughout the tournament. Especially if line shopping with six or seven sportsbooks offering this market.

CONGRATS! 😀 PP.
YOU HAVE WON €275.00

(W) Michail Antonio 1 or more headed shots 9/2
on target
#WhatOddsPaddy - Shots On Target Specials
- West Ham v Leicester
20:01 23 August 2021

Stake   Returns
€50.00   €275.00

Props and Derivative Betting

Michael Antonio was mispriced in the prop markets with one sportsbook at the beginning of the 2022 English Premier League season. He was 9/2 to have a header on target and 4/1 to score from a header in two separate markets. It wasn't a "palp" as such, but something went wrong somewhere. This is just some insight into how inefficient these markets can be and shows how little effort that can go into them.

Antonio was 11/4 for two shots on target compared to 6/5 elsewhere. The 4/1 for a headed goal was a horrendous price by the way.

Antonio was playing the central striking role, and this is possibly another case of him being priced up on figures he collated when playing in a wider position and during the quiet covid period. If you'd been watching him prior, you'd have known how good these bets were. You won't get large stakes on these types of bets, but you can make up for that in volume and expected value.

CONGRATS! 😀 PP.
YOU HAVE WON €330.00
W Michail Antonio   10/1
   Player To Have 3 Or More Shots On Target -
   West Ham v Leicester
   20:01 23 August 2021

Stake   Returns
€30.00   €330.00

CONGRATS! 😀 PP.
YOU HAVE WON €281.25
W Michail Antonio   11/4
   Player To Have 2 Or More Shots On Target -
   West Ham v Leicester
   20:01 23 August 2021

Stake   Returns
€75.00   €281.25

The next match he was evens for two shots on target and 5/2 for a header on target. He was 5/1 for a headed goal with the same firm. The first match was home vs Leicester - to home vs Crystal Palace a few days later. This also shows how supposed supremacy can be over factored into the odds, compiler, or algorithm consensus (usually) being that Antonio is unlikely to get as many shots vs Leicester. This isn't always the case however and often the likes of Leicester or teams high in the xG (expected goals) metric are overvalued. In gameweek ten Westham were home to Tottenham, the exact equivalent of Leicester at the time. Antonio was priced at 11/10 for two shots on target as opposed to the 11/4 earlier in the season. This is a truer reflection of his fair price to have two shots on target and it was now backed up by recent data.

Why was he priced this way? Basically, the updated prior data from the current rather than the previous season now more accurately portrayed his true chance. The data used at the start of the campaign may have been from the previous season which was a massive outlier due to the no fans during Covid. This is an example of using Bayesian Inference or reasoning skills to exploit inefficiencies in the betting markets which do not adjust for these sorts of variables quickly enough. Sometimes these markets are used as enhanced odds gimmicks and you must beware.

For example:

Harry Kane was 7/2 for a header on target in a game with a certain bookmaker. It was 9/2 'powered up' - max bet 20. I bet this and the price was amended to 7/2 in its "powered up" state, claiming the previous normal price was 11/4. The same thing happened with Virgil Van Dijk that day in a Liverpool game. What other industry would they get away with that sort of shenanigans in?

The importance of line shopping

It's quite an eyeopener when shopping around these markets individually in sportsbooks. IE: not on an odds comparison service. It's a bit of work and can be mentally draining but it's certainly worth the effort. The discrepancy in prices across the boards can be substantial. If we take three sportsbooks who offer these markets and compare prices against one another, we often see a wide range of odds.

For example: Antonio was 6/5 with Sky for two shots on target versus Leicester which is around what I made it. He was around 2/1 with Hills, then 11/4 with Paddies. Depending on the prop market, the bigger the prices, the bigger the potential outliers.

If we look at the goal from outside the box markets and check three individual firm's prices, we might see something like 8/1, 14/1 and 25/1 on the same player. We often see this. Usually, the fair price is around the middle price in these scenarios but sometimes it can be towards the lower price point meaning there's huge expected value in these bets by playing books off against one another. **This is called Line Shopping** and is one of the most important aspects of professional or more serious betting. It's not complicated, in fact it's trivial after a while.

If you keep taking the best price or close to it you can essentially play in the markets vig free, or to a very low margin / hold percentage. The new buzzword for this is "**synthetic hold**". Serious bettors in Europe, mainly the UK and Ireland, have been using odds comparison services religiously to line shop or price compare from the early days.

Football lines in the big markets such as the win-draw-win and Totals are dictated by the Asian markets and plenty of copying goes on over in the European sportsbooks. Books like Pinnacle play their part also. Props are outsourced to third parties and copied in some quarters and are very exploitable. There will be lower limits in play and restrictions will come quite easily but they are worth it, and fun!

Props to Ibrahima Konate

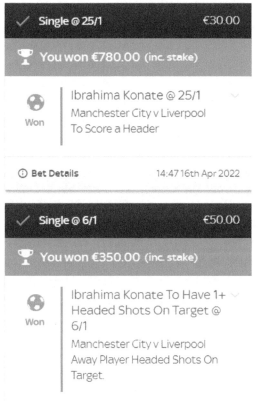

When Ibrahima Konate signed for Liverpool, I told a few of the guys to keep an eye out for him in the air from set pieces. It didn't quite happen for him straight away margin, wasn't confident attacking set pieces in the beginning, and wasn't starting many games. He is an absolute beast in the air.

Prices will drift if he's not scoring which is the upside of some losing bets early doors on a specific angle.

Some firms will wrongly have this type of bet featured in an odds boost if it's flavour of the hour, thinking it's just a random streak. It isn't, that's a mistake. This is what happened when Liverpool played Man City in the FA Cup Semi in 2022. Konate was just coming off the back of a two-legged Champions League quarter final in which he scored a header from a set piece (at a big price) in each leg vs Benfica.

What tends to happen is that against stronger teams, prices will be bigger. This can be flawed logic and is down to raw data compiled on defence strength, supremacy and goals conceded from set pieces etc. This is where line shopping really pays off. Konate was a huge price in a couple of places compared to others (above) to score from a header and for a headed shot on target.

He was 40s for two headed shots on target.

Win   Return + 725.00 €

16 Apr 14:51   Single

Man City vs Liverpool   WIN ↑
To Score a Header
Ibrahima Konate @ 28/1

Virgil van Dijk was half his price, when on this occasion Konate was more likely in both markets to come good. Don't underestimate the power of confidence in football. Konate is simply better in the air attacking set pieces than big Virge but the data did not yet reflect this. In the match following, Konate's prices had still not been amended. A few days later at home to Man UTD, he was 25s to net from a header. The 7/2 for one headed shot on target was lowered quite a bit from 6/1 but he was still priced bigger than Virgil Van Dijk in all these markets.

Goal Scorer betting in Football

The first thing to realise is that the **anytime goal scorer** odds you see in the sportsbooks or on comparison sites are often compiled by a third-party provider rather than the traders at the individual firms. It's not always the case, but many of the big-name brands are supplied by B2B odds consultancy companies. The sportsbook traders can add their margins and adjust to cater for whatever type of clientele they have.

These margins in the **goal scorer markets** are applied mostly to the players at the top of the market - the big-name strikers, and then get gradually thinner as we go down the list. It's usually wise to avoid the biggest names if you are looking to profit long term in first or anytime goal scorer markets. All the value is further down the betting.

Supremacy, goals per minutes ratio, and percentage weight of team goals are some of the main variables incorporated into the models and algorithms churning out **goal scorer betting** odds. Subjective opinion will also be used to adjust the prices in circumstances such as where significant team news or players changing positions are involved.

It's the latter where we can find the real edge. You'll need to be quick to act if some significant team news breaks to nab the best prices on possible replacements as books are also quick to react, especially in the bigger leagues. Situations do arise when certain players will be playing different roles which are not really picked up on by the market.

One example of this is **Doucoure for Everton under Rafa Benitez in 2021**.

In the season previous, Doucoure sat deep in the midfield and didn't see much action in the final third. Under Rafa he operated in a more forward role where he was urged to get into the box, with Allan playing the holding role. This resulted in several assists/goals/ shots on target for Doucoure early season, all at value prices way above the true odds.

Similarly, Reese James was playing an advanced wing back role for Chelsea under Thomas Tuchal, whereas he was more of a full back under Lampard. This led to James finding himself in the box with goal scoring opportunities more often and making some easy assists. Early season you could take advantage of some tasty prices until the data caught up. It's swings and roundabouts though, his price will inflate and deflate depending on a player's most recent form and data.

We saw the same with Denzel Dumfries for Holland in Euro 2021. Dumfries was being priced up in the anytime scorer market like a full back, and he scored in both Holland's opening two games at double figure prices. His role was more like that of a wide man in the front 3. He was also awarded man of the match in these two games at 25/1 which I talk about further down.

"First or anytime goal scorer betting markets are there to be exploited but only if you know what you're doing"

Predicting game patterns or taking notes from watching games can allow you to spot opportunities and angles when no info will be available to odds compilers or layers.

This is easier said than done and requires much experience of watching football, but it's time worth investing.

We can see that generally the traders apply most of their margins to the favourites as they are the players that will attract the most money and bets. This leaves the market open to exploitation further down. Some of these prices will offer value if you can find an angle such as a midfielder playing a more forward role, or a key defender getting injured in the warmup.

Where to bet goal scorer markets

In terms of prices, I suggest not betting until late. We tend to see the lesser names drift or at least stay the same closer to the kick-off. On the exchanges after the team news is released, we can see big drifts on players. Around twenty-five, to ten minutes before the game starts, we are likely to see the best prices on the betting exchange. If you're betting at the sportsbooks, make sure to shop around for the best anytime goal scorer prices as the odds can differ significantly.

Man of the Match Betting

The man of the match markets have been some of the most mispriced markets and most profitable for me over the course of my betting career. The dynamics of the markets can differ depending on the league or tournament they are being offered in. There can be big pricing discrepancies and errors across the books. Unfortunately, the man of the match betting product is getting harder and harder to source and only a handful of books generally price up (at the period of writing).

We usually see a man of the match book priced up to around 130% where the market percentage is still exploitable despite the overround. This is basically a reflection of the lack of confidence traders have in the market. The higher the overrounds the more certain sections of the market can be beaten, as a rule, contrary to popular theory. **Attack markets with higher overrounds**. There's a reason why they are high.

Antepost markets can also fall under this bracket. These MOTM markets will often have the squads involved and a few of them will be suspended or injured so most of the margin can be eroded straight away if you're savvy enough to see it. Some markets can even be over-broke, and if you can line shop, you might find yourself with some huge mathematical edges.

As alluded to above, **Denzel Dumfries** was on the team sheet for the Dutch as a right back for the Dutch Euro 2021 matches. He was priced up at around 10/1 to score anytime from the bare numbers which is about right for an attacking full back you might estimate if your domain knowledge is up to scratch. What happens though if he plays more as a winger or forward on the flank and gets himself into plenty of great positions and even scores a goal? Usually nothing, as it's not reflected in the long-term data used for pricing. He did score in this example, and he was priced up the same for matchday 2.

The same thing happened again - he got man of the match in both games as well as scoring in each. He was priced at 25/1 plus for MOTM if you shopped around. In terms of attacking these markets, it's sometimes very easy to exploit. The most important factor to consider is who is choosing the man of the match award. Bias is a huge variable in play.

In the English Premier league Gary Neville used to always give the man of the match award to David Silva or Vincent Kompany if he was doing comms on their matches. Alan Smith was another big fan of David Silva and if he had any sort of a decent game, he'd often get the gong when Smith was in charge of picking the award winner. When Jamie Redknapp was in the studio for a Chelsea game it was uncanny how often Cousin Frank Lampard or friend John Terry got the award!

LOGIC WINS.

Be smart, it's not rocket science. If you were to dutch bet Lampard and Terry for man of the match every time Chelsea played and Redknapp was about, you'd be quids in. You get good prices on all players in this man of the match market - none of this bias stuff is factored in.

If we take the big football tournaments - the World Cup or the Euros, a few firms price this market up on most of the games. It's important to see how the voting takes place - is it a fan vote, or is it decided by a FIFA representative?

I remember one time it was a fan vote in the World Cup and the Nigerian goalkeeper got man of the match at double figure prices in all Nigeria's group games, win, or lose. It was hilarious. Bear in mind keepers rarely win MOTM. They were beaten 3-0 in one of the group games and he still got the gong - he was worshipped back home in Nigeria.

It's similar with players like Ronaldo and Messi and you could get strong prices around 3/1 on these guys. Literally if their teams won, they'd get the fan vote, maybe even if they didn't. Sometimes MOTM prices will adjust for the latter rounds when books become aware of these trends, but they never seem to learn anything before the next tournament comes up and it's silly season all over again in the beginning.

Let's talk about golf, baby....

"Ultimately, it's a matter of judgement. Numbers never give you an answer. They give you an assistance towards an answer, and then other things become relevant" - Keith Elliot

The theory behind Course Fit in Golf

In my first book "Angles and Edges', we talked about the wind in golf betting and concluded with a rule of 0.1 strokes difference per 1mph of wind, with that number getting gradually bigger at winds of over around 25mph. I mentioned the word Bayesian and there is a general underlying theme throughout this book of what's known as Bayesian Inference. Later, we will get stuck into that with a chapter but for now I just want to give you a little example.

The most obvious one is my thoughts on course fit. Some of you will be aware that I've been banging on about course fit for over ten years now online. It's such a simple concept yet so underutilised in golf betting and concepts like it in sports betting in general. Course fit is an example of what's known as the conditional probability - the thing that changes each player's actual true chances of success the most from week to week in golf tournaments or general sports markets.

I've been adopting a Moneyball and sabermetrics style approach to golf betting since the beginning. Essentially, I've been using strokes gained before it was a known concept, along with player profiling in key stats, metrics and trend analysis. The only thing was, not being a modeller, I didn't have actual definitive numbers. With the birth of strokes gained and advanced statistics, I built my course fit and progressive form models to put numbers on my theories. Let the quote below sink in as it's more appropriate than you could imagine.

"The more you see it the more you understand it" - Ted Scott on Augusta

What exactly is course fit in golf betting terms?

Course fit is so underrated by the market. It's the one area where you can get a real edge on what's not built into the prices, and every week we can narrow down the field significantly using this concept. A strong course fit will equal as many as two strokes per round, more in the case of some outliers such as Bryson at Caves Valley on a soft day. Bryson missed a five-foot putt here in the BMW Championship on the last hole to lose out on shooting a 59. We saw what his power off the tee can do to a long track with wide landing areas and little trouble. If we consider Dustin Johnson playing without his driver as he did at Liberty National in the Northern Trust 1st round in 2021, how many strokes per round would this cost him?

Imagine it was Augusta where power is a prerequisite. Now take the wedge out of his bag. Approach proximity with the wedge and length off the tee are two of DJs strong points. If we disable these weapons at a course that demands class in these areas, how many shots will it cost him over the tournament?

"Course fit is the golden goose in golf betting"

DJ at Augusta is what I refer to as a strong course fit as opposed to a track where he wouldn't gain much advantage vs the field with driver or his wedges - somewhere like Harbour Town, which I'd refer to as a neutral course for him. We can use the strokes gained statistics to predict who might go well on specific courses, finding the key metrics for that particular course from past editions of the tournament. This is course fit - individual skill sets for particular courses.

Strokes gained in golf betting explained

Strokes gained in golf is a relatively new concept to measure the performance of golfers. Variance in golf is huge and final round or tournament scores don't tell the whole story. With strokes gained we can measure expectancy and use it to predict potential future performance vs the golf betting markets, which will be weighted towards the overlying data such as finishing positions.

" The PGA Tour has calculated the average number of strokes needed to hole out from every distance and location on the courses. These averages were calculated in one-inch increments on the greens and one-yard increments off the green and are used to create baselines of the average tour performance. With the baseline as the foundation the tour can calculate the probability of an outcome from any distance and location " - PGA Tour

---

The way the golf betting markets work are with margins added that usually combine to about 55 - 60%. Much of this percentage margin is built into the front tiers of the market with a theoretical 1.5 - 4% hold (margin) on some of the big boys (if we compare to exchange prices). There is also plenty to add up on the no hopers down the pack.

If we focus more on tier two and tier three of the market, we are operating in a much more level playing field. The winner often comes from here. Concentrating on this section also lessens the variance.

Progressive form in golf

For a further edge in golf betting, we can look for something I call progressive form to add to course fit. I also created a mathematical model on "Nicspicks" to rate players for progressive form, which picks up on the golfers who are trending in the right direction. They may have exponentially improved recent form figures, or they might be making lots of birdies but having a nightmare on a few holes each week. They could be putting three good rounds together but struggling on Sundays. All these things lead to pricing inefficiencies the next week in the golf betting markets when you are looking to weigh up a golfer's true chance. The same concepts generally apply to most sports and betting markets.

Rory McIlroy lay-up example - how probability is misunderstood

Rory had a choice between going for the par five 18th in two or laying up on the last hole in Dubai. Getting it done quickly was 60% likely vs a 35% likelihood doing it slowly, using Rory specific conditional probability. Using field averages would give you the wrong percentages. He could also do what Lucas Herbert once did and get up and in for par if he goes in water, while going for it on his second shot.

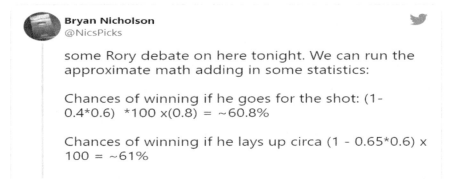

Bryan Nicholson
@NicsPicks

some Rory debate on here tonight. We can run the approximate math adding in some statistics:

Chances of winning if he goes for the shot: (1-0.4*0.6) *100 x(0.8) = ~60.8%

Chances of winning if he lays up circa (1 - 0.65*0.6) x 100 = ~61%

There was plenty of back and forth on Twitter debating whether Rory was right to go for this shot or not, and this is the perfect example of noone having a barney gumble about probability. The maths above shows he had basically the same win chance either way.

Streelman and the Masters par 3 contest

You might be tempted to have a bit of a chuckle here but the Masters par 3 contest used to be a fantastic event and market for betting. Why? Simple - It's all about exploiting flaws in the markets. With little signal producing data to go on, the prices were very inefficient for this event. Betting limits were not too high for said reason but you could get a few quid on it if you were savvy. The prices would not incorporate a lot of qualitative estimates that golf betting experts were privy to. In the earlier days this competition was more serious but as the years went on it became more of a fun event with kids and caddies hitting some shots for the players. This led to an auto disqualification and thus a losing bet. Some players would take it a lot more seriously and the trick was to locate and target these golfers.

The market was priced up on the quality of the player - correlating to where they were in the actual Masters main market. This is wrong on many levels. There's only one stat worth looking at here and there's not a whole lot of difference between all the players in this stategory. You should have been able to throw a blanket around all the prices if making a true book. This is a similar inefficiency to the one the First Round Leader market had for years.

My strategy was to target the better wedge players at high prices. This data was easily found on the PGA Tour site: 100-125 yards was around the distance of most of the holes. The guys not so experienced at the Masters were the guys less likely to have kids or girlfriends caddying - the more nervous and or more serious /

competitive guys, and these would usually prove the golfers who would play it out and often win. **Kevin Streelman** was 50s-66 the year he beat Camillo Villegas in the playoff and it made for an interesting Wednesday evening. Villegas, if I recall correctly, had some water trouble on the extra hole(s). It wasn't the only year I had success and indeed the winner at a good price in this event. Back then pictures were hard to get - if you could get them at all - so there wasn't a lot of opportunity to see what was going on behind the scenes if you were compiling odds. Not a lot of effort went into pricing this. It was just a gimmick to whet the appetite for the real Masters betting. Over the years more and more players started messing and the kids and girlfriends were competing more, so it became a nightmare to price and offer a market on, unfortunately.

James Hart Du Preez exposes the Models

James Hart Du Preez was one absolute classic example of how you can use conditional probability (or common sense to the lesser mortal) and a bit of deeper knowledge and information to beat the market and odds which are compiled on what I call 'rule of thumb mathematics'. First of all, at this time, James was a little known professional golfer outside of South Africa, his circle, or maybe to a small collection of avid golf bettors or enthusiasts. There was little data to show his skills or ability and he hadn't yet really performed on the big stage.

So is it any surprise then that given what form he did have documented was crap, he was priced up at 750 to 1000/1 for the Steyn City Classic on the DP World Tour (or European Tour). For the serious golf bettors with course knowledge also in tow, and armed with the info that Du Preez was **arguably the biggest hitter on the golf circuit at the time** (he can routinely drive not far off 400 yards), this was a serious opportunity, albeit speculative.

Pos		Country	Player Name			Today		Hole	Score	R1	R2
1	-	🏴	NORRIS, Shaun ⬭ODYSSEY		⊳	-		12:41	-18	64	62
2	-	🏴	DU PREEZ, James Hart			-		12:41	-15	63	66
3	-	🏴	BURMESTER, Dean		⊳	-		12:31	-13	66	65
4	-	🇩🇰	HANSEN, Joachim B.			-		12:21	-12	68	64
	-	🇩🇰	SODERBERG, Sebastian			-		12:21	-12	65	67
	-	🏴	BEKKER, Oliver		⊳	-		12:31	-12	69	63
7	-	🇩🇰	MØLLER, Niklas Nørgaard			-		11:51	-11	66	67

James Hart Du Preez signed for -15 after two rounds of the Steyn City Classic with a power display

The course was Steyn City, a similar track to Serengeti. It's open, exposed, and to add fuel to the fire, soft conditions came into play to drive the narrative. Bear in mind only a small percentage of people would have been running this angle as James quite simply was still an unknown, not to mention the course was also unknown to the masses of golf bettors.
All these variables at the time were not factored into the prices, especially for openers. They rarely are, not accurately anyway. Du Preez alongside Sean Norris blitzed the field at the halfway stage.

The thinking here for the top pros was that Du Preez could absolutely mash this course apart on this particular week. It won't always happen, but it won't be a coincidence when it does. Being armed with this info can lead to books like this, even for small outlay
:

Winner	Each Way - 10 ...	3rd Round Le...	Top 5 Finish	Top 10 Finish	Top 20 Finish

Going In-Play ● | Cash Out i | Rules | ✦ Pin   Matched: **EUR 202,462**

Selections	141.8%		Back all	Lay all	
Shaun Norris €397.26	2.1 €165	2.18 €84	2.2 €2	2.24 €354	2.26 €87
Dean Burmester €168.50	7 €10	7.4 €129	7.6 €9	8 €14	8.2 €18
James Hart du Preez €7,668.50	5.9 €24	13 €54	15.5 €49	17 €1	17.5 €42
Oliver Bekker €168.50	15 €46	17 €45	17.5 €1	18 €59	18.5 €2
Joachim B. Hansen €168.50	18 €8	18.5 €4	19 €38	21 €2	22 €5
Wilco Nienaber €168.50	10 €19	21 €11	22 €41	600 €1	
Romain Langasque €168.50	17.5 €40	23 €20	24 €26	34 €10	42 €59
Sebastian Soderberg €168.50	8.2 €10	25 €46	26 €51	44 €27	
George Coetzee €168.50	30 €22	32 €8	34 €2		
Hennie Du Plessis €168.50	26 €27	34 €30	36 €2	50 €28	70 €2
Thriston Lawrence €168.50	32 €1	34 €1	36 €27	700 €1	820 €11
Mikko Korhonen €168.50	32 €22	40 €5	42 €21	60 €28	70 €1
Niklas Norgaard Moller €168.50	40 €19	44 €7	46 €17	75 €22	

There's a big freeroll on Du Preez here, and he also took the 1st round lead solo at -9 and was a whopping 250/1 to 300/1 ew to do so. There wasn't a lot invested in this tournament pre-tourney on Betfair. It's a low risk potential high reward strategy, with a big +EV bet. James was actually -11 with two holes to go in the first round. What happens with the golf odds in play is that between rounds the prices are like a derivative price from the pre-tourney odds combined with the score the player shoots in each round.

It won't be adjusted for conditional variables unless of course he's absolutely smashed in by bettors. This means the odds will often remain wrong and sometimes very wrong and we as astute bettors can take advantage. All markets work like this, all sports. The concept of the maths used is flawed when looking at each different market individually, as I have and will repeat throughout this book.

Bryan Nicholson @NicsPicks · 6h ···

James Hart Du Preez crushing the models and showing the limitations of quantitative algos and rule of thumb formulas at the half way stage of Steyn City. 1000> 7s and still far too big on this *bombers* track

◯   ⇄   ♡ 4   ↑   ⫴

Du Preez had come all the way into 7s from 1000s after he finished his 2nd round. Sean Norris made him drift back out a bit after carding a round two -10 in the early late draw. Pre-tournament favourite Dean Burmester helped push him back out a little too.

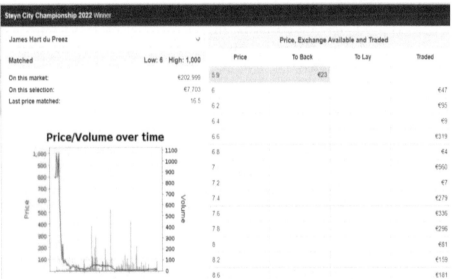

James Du Preez betfair price graph for the first 36 holes of the Steyn City Champs

In the end Du Preez finished 5th for a huge 200/1 place payout on the EW part of the bet. Add that to his 250 to 1 (300 to 1 in some sportsbooks) first round leader win and various other subsidiary markets like a top 20 at 33/1. He also traded at single figures from 1000.0 pre-event.

"Statistically you can have an algorithm and say it doesn't affect anything but believe me as a golfer it's all about the psyche at this level "

- Paul McGinley on momentum

Heuristics, shortcuts and the betting markets

In sports betting markets, we are often now working with universal algorithmic based pricing. The maths behind this pricing can be described as heuristics. I refer to the betting markets and how they can work for both bookmakers and punters as the Blackbox Paradox. In maths, a heuristic is a rule of thumb method that is used to solve a maths problem - a method used by students to problem-solve.

When I look at the betting markets in the previous chapters I see heuristics everywhere. I also see huge potential to exploit the maths behind these markets - like playing against guys grinding twenty tables in poker, using rules of thumb in each and every hand. The reality is every hand is different. The result of people firing up more tables is usually a lower win rate but possibly a higher bankroll due to volume.

If I was to try and price up a golf tournament on the Korn Ferry or the Challenge Tour using the rankings on the OWGR and official sites, I could do a job. It would be a job full of heuristics though and I'm aware I'd be completely open to exploitation to golf bettors who know all the players and how good they really are at ceiling, average and floor level. My prices, taken individually, could be picked apart.

Bryan Nicholson @NicsPicks · Mar 23

Replying to @Golfpunter1

Exactly. I call it the market black box. Unless you can actually visually equate the numbers with what's going on in the sports/dynamics then you'll never be able to spot patterns with true signal, and thus prices can still be off by quite a bit vs true probabilities

♡   ⇄   ♡   ⬆   ⅲ

"At its most basic a heuristic is a shortcut in problem solving - a rule for reducing the number of mental operations taken to solve a problem. Students can use heuristics on their own to help identify and solve a maths problem"

Heuristics in Maths and Betting

We are talking about mathematical heuristics now. They say trial and error is a heuristic, but over a big sample you can learn what works, I think. BODMAS in maths is a heuristic.

- Rule of thumb
- Educated guess
- Intuitive judgement
- Common sense
- Algorithm
- Formulae
- Model
- Back testing

What happens in the betting markets is the traders and odds compilers who are so used to putting these markets together, given the rule of thumb maths behind them, is that they can forget the maths is only a guide - a rule of thumb that is efficient over the average of a large sample to give out **implied** probabilities. This is precisely the premise of heuristics.

In poker the solvers make assumptions and place everyone in the same population. It works with casino gaming as everything is like a robot or random number generator (RNG). That's far from the case in real life sports betting and probabilities where the actual fair odds or true probabilities doesn't necessarily reflect the odds implied by sports markets at all.

What are Odds? Odds are **implied** probabilities. Emphasis on the word implied. Looking back over the sample as a whole and seeing point 'b' was reached from point 'a' at a relatively straight line, they could be forgiven for thinking it was quite a dull process.

That's looking from outside the "black box" though. If you are inside manning the controls and a part of the cogs, the sum of all parts, you might notice, is a lot more volatile.

Trial and error - empirical observation and the rule of thumb

You can't ever understand inside the black box of the betting markets without learning empirically. That means through empirical observation and trial and error, which translates in English to: make bets and lots of them and watch them play out over and over.

Was your thinking correct? How did the markets move and react through the few hours or days around the bet, and how did the lines adjust in play? In poker I learned from playing tens, then hundreds of thousands of hands. I didn't need a solver to tell me the sizing, it was me and a few guys like me who in the end told the solver what sizings to make. Someone needed to influence the programming for the range and equity software and solvers, right?

Black Box Paradox

Understanding the sports betting markets is the key to beating the sports betting markets. People are seeing and trusting the bare results or the input and output data without understanding what's going on inside the "black box" (essentially the dynamics of the market).

Those who know the "why" will question the efficiency of the market a lot more. These days people who like using heuristics (consciously or subconsciously) are inclined to take what a model says as gospel without questioning it. What might look like an efficient market from the outside may not be when you look at the sum of all its parts. It's the same in fave - longshot bias academic studies - they don't tell the whole story when you just back test a load of data.

Let's imagine one thousand planes flying from 'A' to 'B' and all planes land safely. If you look at a record of the flights, you'll see nothing wrong - all efficient flights with no trouble are what you conclude. But what if you investigated the *actual* Black Boxes and then realised that one hundred of those flights had serious trouble in the air?

High Level of Granularity, Beating Vig with Conditional Probability

The most popular form of betting, especially for the pros and more serious bettors are pickems on the spread, evenly matched money lines or over / under totals at 10/11 (-110) a piece. This is the standard betting market where the bookmakers think (or perceive the public to think) it is a very equal affair. Anticipated money coming in will be approximately evenly distributed and a proportional margin can be applied.

Easy right? As a trader, just apply this equal margin of the standard 2.4% each side and pull the ~ 4.5% vig or juice (or commission). Maybe it **is** easy but here's how this is also very exploitable in the right circumstances on the punter side....

An example popped up on Twitter where an apparent slightly controversial question was posed by an official PGA golf source. But should it have been controversial?
It went like this: Would you rather have a breaking two-foot putt to win a golf tournament or a straight 9-footer?

While the obvious answer is the two-footer, the percentages are not quite as far apart as the masses assume. *The actual* answer might be the two-footer, but it isn't as cut and dried as replies suggest. Intuitively most people will be way off when estimating probabilities of this type (or any type). There are some funny stories I can tell but that's for another day, or book! This concept is also a great example to use practically against the betting markets and I give an example below of a real betting analogy. The average hole out percentage for an elite pro golfer might be 50% from eight feet but if we were to theoretically add in a high level of granularity into our decision process on when and who to bet, with the ability to be completely selective, this means big potential profit. *Average* is the key word.

Bryan Nicholson
@NicsPicks

...

Here is an interesting 1. The average make % of putts from 8' on the big boy tours is 50%. If you offered me just 10/11 (-110) on *any* individual 8 footers I wanted, being selective, theoretically (if I had access to key information in real time) I could take you apart

I'm using a golf example here but it's the same methodology and theory for any pickems or two-way markets at the same odds offered. The bookie has his inbuilt commission and if I was to wager on -110 odds repeatedly on a 50% shot (make or miss the putt in this case) which is what is implied here, I lose x amount.

What if I add in the following factors?

1. Quality of putter
2. Grass type
3. Slope and speed of putt

Expected value (EV) Calculator	
Stake	100
Probability of loss	0.41
Probability of win	0.59
Potential profit	91
EV ($)	12.69

I'd expect to hit anywhere between 58-63% rather than the 52.4% needed to break even against the vig. This equates to a ROI of 8-18% long term.

If we were to make it simple by just choosing putts on greens with 11-12 stimp and putts with little breaks, meaning we must start it within one inch of the hole maximum, I'd expect to beat the odds when being selective with my knowledge of the player's putting tendencies. Doing this would see the hole out percentage from 8' something closer to 60%. We need to break it down individually rather than have all putts piled into the same big data average population of the mythical (average) 50% figure. This is the power of selectivity for sports bettors.

We have a 60%-win rate on a 10/11 shot through conditional probability (or pure logic as I sometimes call it). What happens in these types of markets is the bookies win, as do the small selection of smart players. Remember bookies will ban or limit the smart guys that do this stuff, or they would be destroyed by a conglomerate of shrewd operators.

If we take every match, game, market, and sport individually there will be many instances where adding in this level of granularity will enlighten you to the fact it's really a 60/40 proposition towards one side (sometimes more) rather than the 50% to 50% implied by the odds. Several of the more obscure (but most important when it comes to finding an edge) variables won't be factored into the pricing medium.

The Bayesian Bettor vs the Frequentist Modeller, and Pinny

The Frequentist method of statistics never estimates the probability of the unknown, while the Bayesian method uses probabilities borne of data and hypothesis testing or empirical observation. Frequentist methods do not demand construction of a prior, rather they depend on the probabilities implied from data analysis. Betting markets are formed predominantly on Frequentist probabilities.

If we watch the UFC, there are certain fighters known for gassing after two or three rounds. Over their careers they might only have an average of twenty fights each but every fight where they went over three rounds they gassed and got knocked out or submitted. Would this trend change the more fights they had? Like the Mon Mome example, probably not, unless there had been some sort of significant outlier at play.

If we were to put that into practice with two people:

A.   Bayesian theorist (logic and reasoning to predict probability as a degree of belief)
B.   Frequentist numbers man (relies on large sample data to interpret probabilities)

Let's say person A was a regular watcher of the UFC and knew from using his actual eyes and memory that the above was the case with a particular fighter with a very strong win loss record. Person B was just crunching the data and knew how often the fighter won and lost but had no idea from the data how or why (the black box paradox). You offer both guys 5/1 on the fighter in question's opponent winning the match given he's tough and has never been knocked out in 3 rounds. **This is the key conditional**. This means the opponent will likely take our fighter with the great record into gas out territory, and now he's vulnerable. Person A bites your hand off for the 5/1 believing the gassy fighter will tire fast after round 3. Person B says no he doesn't want the bet as the stats say it's neutral EV.

Who wins long term?

The Bayesian wins all hands down. We might be working off an EV of as high as 70% backing the guy that doesn't tire, yet the trader using the frequentist method thinks it's a neutral EV bet.

Marco Blume, Pinnacle Sports director talks about qualitative analysis and says how it's strictly Bayesian style thinking behind the data science and pricing up at Pinny. They have three teams of experts in: risk, modelling (quant) and in the domain knowledge, and marry all together. Then they put together decent lines, with low enough limits and allow the big players to move them to efficiency, and then loosen the limits. That's the pinnacle business model. High limits and small margins due to accurate odds or lines.

He talks about the "known knowns, known unknowns, and unknown unknowns" when referencing small samples and events with no real data, and how you can estimate (Bayesian style) accurate probabilities.

For example:

1. Germany vs Uruguay were playing a football match when they hadn't played each other in twenty years
2. Two random sprinters on the street are about to race, when you see one has crutches…

Basically, his point is (like mine) that there is high variance that needs to be ironed out with large samples in truly random events like a coin flip, but sports betting is not truly random and there are many instances where the uncertainty is highly quantifiable in small samples. This is what I often call the logic behind the variables. While watching the games play out, we will see the theoretical profit and loss graph staying much closer on average to the expected EV line, and variance will be less.

When variables are changeable it's a different story to when they are not. True probabilities are up in the air compared to when variables are fixed like in poker odds or roulette or blackjack with multiple decks (no card counting).

Enrico Fermi was a physicist who was known to be able to make good approximate calculations. Some of these later became known as "Fermi Problems" and they are used in interviews for higher intellect jobs. One of these is 'How many piano tuners are there in Chicago?' and 'How much does the Empire State building weigh?'

Conor McGregor was due to fight Floyd Mayweather and there was no data on this available or indeed from similar historic fights, so how does one go about pricing it? There was a good article on Pinnacle Sports blog that used the Fermi Piano Tuner problem method - using qualitative analysis to solve this problem. You break down the problem into stages using your best guestimate of each piece of the puzzle.

Soft vs sharp books

Similar to the way poker has gone, closing line value (CLV) has become the in thing. Playing off sharp books and attacking the soft books lines is a strategy many big players are using, and it is also one that can be automated using value betting software.
It's not a new strategy, I love to play the books off against one another in obscure markets, usually prop markets that are not on Betfair and have a minimal showing on Oddschecker or other odds comparison services. You'll be surprised at the array of odds you can get by checking the sportsbooks individually. The true price is often in the middle of the range and sometimes at the lower end, so by picking off these numbers you can do well. We must be wary of account limiting.

The models behind the madness

Cognitive bias dictates that everyone thinks their model is great and can basically predict the future of sporting events. The reality is most of them are useless. No one wants to hear that about their own model but the reason why the majority in the long term won't make money using them is that they have nothing to measure their outputs against in terms of watching and having an intuitive feel for the true probabilities. Like in poker, sports bettors are being brainwashed into thinking these models are the be all and end all, but there's no substitute for understanding the 'why' behind the data, and thus have the ability to adapt to different factors.

I've been watching golf for so long that I understand how often things are likely to happen and I can use that to back up stats or dismiss the stats. There is a small percentage of people who have a unique ability to visually equate what they see into numbers and probabilities. The whole basis of my approach is empirical.

Models are only as good as their inputs, "sh!t in, sh!t out" as they say. This obviously isn't the case for all, and the best models out there can do serious damage. The key to models is obviously using the correct variables and metrics and weighting them efficiently in the algorithm.

"SH!T IN SH!T OUT"

Remember this if you ever find yourself running 5,000 simulations. Although it seems great, you're probably wasting your time if you want to create an edge and make money. If you actually understand your sports and markets and how to weigh the variables properly, by all means give it a shot. You can do it simply in excel for starters. You need to have what I call gambling smarts to be able to fine tune any model you are involved with. If you have both skill sets this is great and you could build a highly accurate predictive model.

"I think one of my strengths is I know my weaknesses" -
Alan "Dink" Denkenson (Lay the Favourite)

A big part of the motivation for this book was to show people without coding or modelling skills that beating the markets can be done the old skool way (the best way), despite the inevitable takeover of AI. I witnessed it in poker and the same thing is happening. Poker is still far from dead and there has been a massive influx of new beginner players in more recent years.

I want to teach you how to think critically. Note and study the performance of your bets to help understand if you were on the right track with your thinking. A lot of models in machine learning are centred around the mean and can be easily exploited. I talk about the clustering illusion concept later in the book, and the fact clusters do appear over or under their baselines for good reason.

Trackers and simulators are becoming more common in the era of In-play betting. Sports betting "HUDs" are now a thing and companies like IMG arena are bringing a real time data product to the internet. The days of court siding may be numbered. This is where teams of people are at the sporting event dripping real time data and info back to partners, or maybe even betting themselves.

We are going to see much more of this data driven revolution in the coming years as in-play betting takes over and people migrate to sports betting, in the same way as solvers took over the poker world. IGM has been incorporated into Bet 365s in play betting product in the golf and we can see in real time the shot-by-shot tracking and data coming from the course. This data is ahead of odds moves even on the exchanges so be very careful if betting or trading in running. Plenty of mistakes are also being made with this data and tracking in the earlier days.

Each Way Betting: Place Terms vs Prices

A topic we often see discussed on social media or down the pub amongst friends in betting is whether it's best to take the extra places or the bigger prices. The answer as always in sports betting is it depends on the sport, the market and other variables, but in general, what's best?

Smart people in the game will argue to take the bigger prices: these people will often include the significantly maths oriented, such as traders and market makers. Frequentist statisticians. It's not as simple as that. The theoretical maths is the maths, we can't argue with that. We can work out what each extra place is equivalent to in terms of expected value vs price. Or can we? The maths might be right IF everything is equal, if all is random, like using the analogy of odds in poker where the implied probabilities equal the actual probabilities. Or when using a random number generator.

Is this true in sports betting? Not necessarily.

For example: All golfers are different and taking each market selection on its own merit we need to use conditional probability to form more precise prices for true probabilities. In sports betting we need to weigh up and add in these variables.

When we do this, the dynamic and the maths changes. The implied probabilities don't necessarily match up to the actual probabilities.

Using the golf markets as an example, you might argue that ¼ five places at 100/1 is better than 1/5th eight places at 75/1 given the bigger payouts relative to the places - the lazy maths behind it. But what if the player in question rarely finishes in the top 2-5 places? What if nearly every time he plays well the best he can do is 6th-8th. My records show that a mid to longer odds player is on average ~ 2x more likely to finish in positions 6-8 than 2nd-5th when he places. Check it yourself in the official records.

You are not unlucky betting golf if your player drops a shot late on and fails to place, that's normal, you didn't make the right play. If we add up all the extra place money, we recoup with positions 6-8 onside given a theoretical large sample of bets, that sum added to all places and wins outweighs the money we get back from taking the higher prices and lesser place terms, and thus it is a better +EV bet.

It's not always the case though. We can move to horse racing, and we might like the lesser places at bigger prices. Why? Because a horse dropping a length might be less likely to make a difference to their finishing position, whereas a competing golfer dropping a shot late on will probably move them back four or five spots. If you look at the tweet above or example below you will see you can do the maths on each component of the bet at each set of terms individually and add it all up. You need to estimate how often your selection finishes in each tier of the place positions to do this properly.

Backing a golfer five places is no use if said golfer doesn't have a ceiling high enough to get in that top five a high enough percentage of the time in a much more competitive golf era. The Each Way odds are just **implied** probabilities. I argue that these win and place markets are much more independent than people think. They can't be treated as straight derivatives of the win price, or the concept behind the maths will be flawed.

If a player is 100.0 to win it doesn't automatically make him 9/1 to top 10 - that depends on conditional factors such as the strength and depth of the field and the specific player type in question, and what form he or she is in.

"X% of something is better than y% of nothing"

Consider this:

I repeatedly offer you 12s about a golfer finishing in the top five, knowing he almost never finishes in the top five. Meanwhile I'm taking a cut price 4/1 off someone else on the same golfer finishing in the top eight knowing he's fairly regular in positions 6 - 10. Who is getting the best bet and who is getting mugged off? Only one of us will have money at the end of the year. There's no point taking 12s if you can't realise your equity.

If these golfers were all robots or clones of one another and the uncertainty was completely random, I'd be taking the bad bet. That's the difference. It's not as simple as doing the straight maths saying double the places is equal to twice the probability. The probability of an average pro golfer finishing in the top five is significantly lower than the probability of finishing in positions six through ten, as it's obviously a lot tougher to play the quality of golf needed to get higher up the board for the pros. If we shop around and get 75-80% of the general opening price with extra places (often possible using an odds comparison grid), we can run some numbers and see what happens…

Example: £10 each way on a golfer at 100.0 at ¼ 5 vs £10 each way on the golfer at 80.0 1/5th 8. The true odds are 80.00 in the win market, so we are making 80 each way bets in this example.

Note: there is some subjectivity involved as to how often the golfer would avail of the extra places. This is a guide to portray the extra place hypothesis which I have a long-term sample to refer to.

¼ 5 places 100.0
outlay £1600 (10 x 160 bets)
Win return = 1 win * 100.0 = £1000
Place return: 4 places * 25.0 = £1000
Total return: £2000
Profit: £400

1/5th 8 places 80.0
outlay £1600 (10 x 160 bets)
Win return: 1 win * 80.0 = £800
Place return: 10 places * 16.0 = £1600
Total return = £2400
Profit = £800

Key point here is that place markets should not be straight derivatives of the win market. Shot values and place values differ, as do player tendencies. **We must lineshop to offset the odds and fractional decrease** and that's where some people get confused. Never take lower than around 70% of the general price for extra places as a rule. We are using bayes theorem on top of the normal maths when working out how often the players will fill the extra places. We are trying to look for long odds golfers that are going to outperform their odds longterm and squeeze into those extra places more often than implied. The sum of all this extra place money would outweigh the bigger price winnings on the majority of golfers.

Backing the front of the market would alter the dynamics somewhat.

The golf markets when you line shop for a **synthetic hold** (when you take best price from numerous operators to get rid of theoretical overround) become like a "bad each way" race for the traders when the place side is completely over broke. The favourites are all short prices. If you compare the place only odds you are getting to this EW market (place odds), you'll see significant differences and mathematically the bookmakers can be in a bad spot.

Circa Sports and other Clangers

Note: I wasn't involved personally in these next few bets but listening to podcasts featuring some smart minds in the industry I have come across a few great opportunities and situational exploits that went on. These are along similar lines to how I've gone about beating the markets for almost 20 years.

Circa sports opened with a line of 250 in the total points market for a women's basketball match. They went up early and the line was compiled using historical data. Circa were up first and originated the line. When other books went up, they had set the line much lower - below 200pts.

Circa are an American book that are vocal in the pride they take in accepting bigger bets at their (what they consider) efficient prices, so this *unders* action was apparently hammered on the day. What had happened is that the format of the women's basketball game had changed from the previous season and this factor along with some other dynamics of the season had meant that the game would be a lot more defensive than previously, and the total points were likely to be a lot lower. This again shows the limitations of just using past data.

Here is a betting story recalled by some industry insiders including Matt T:

In 2019 the US Women's soccer team played Thailand in the World Cup. They hammered them 13-0. There was no easing off as the women celebrated every goal with gusto and even the substitutes were gunning to get in on the action. The books have their in-play pricing model and don't tend to deviate from it. Time decay is something they use in updating their line changes. To the trained eye, it was easy to see that this was going to be an absolute rout from early on. Noone really contemplates that the handicap or the total goals line should be more than a few goals. What would often happen is the traders would take some hits and *average in* to recoup losses, but the goals kept coming here with no time for an overhaul of the odds. Industrial Conkers were done.

Leo Messi and Diego Maradona

I came across a few different people who were involved in a bet, some discussing it via Twitter. AKbets was involved IIRC. I knew nothing of it but was a little intrigued with the thinking, if not the narrative, so I looked deeper into the bet. Diego Maradona had passed away and Barcelona were due to play a match vs Osasuna. Leo Messi was 11/1 to be booked anytime.

As I keep preaching in "Hypnotised by Numbers", prices are compiled on data and not too much anymore on subjective opinion or qualitative variables, and this is where the shrewd bettors come in. Messi rarely picks up any bookings. He was 25/1 or thereabouts to pick up the first booking. The thinking here from the guys was that Messi would be wearing something on his t-shirt underneath his jersey in tribute to the late Maradona and if he scored (which he was around 70-75% likely to do, from stats) he would take off his jersey to reveal his message, and then get booked as per the ruling.

He duly obliged, revealing the no.10 shirt of Newell's Old Boys under his jersey following his goal, and picked up the only yellow card of the game.

Let's say Messi was 50% likely to do this if he scored, which seems a fair estimate. That would make the probability of Messi scoring and getting booked: 0.7*0.5 = 0.35. That's 35% likely or around 2/1 as a fair price and books were quoting 11s, as that's the price the more recent historic data churned out in the 'cards' stats. This is a brilliant bet.

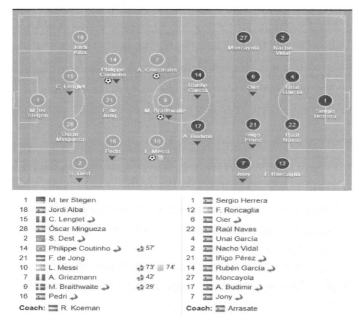

These kinds of situations pop up more often than you might think. If you want to go and bet in play you may find even more of them. Be patient and wait to strike and pick off these kinds of bets.

Variables like this will very rarely be factored into the odds in the new, big data era of bookmaking.

Closing Line Value & the Efficient Market Hypothesis

Closing Line Value or CLV is just a newer term for an old concept - amongst any kind of serious bettors - of measuring your performance in sports betting by how much you beat the close by. It's a way to track performance like HUDs in poker. There are many flaws in this practice. Closing line value is like expected value in terms of percentages. Bear in mind both are theoretical in terms of actual value obtained. The difference is that expected value is the percentage difference between the odds you take and the fair price you originate. Closing line value is the difference between the odds you take and the closing line (odds at start of event). Neither line may be reflective of the actual true odds - that depends on the efficiency of the market or your skill at compiling prices, respectively.

To express CLV as a percentage we have a formula which works similarly to the formula for expected value (EV)

(X-Y/Y) *100, where X is decimal odds taken, and Y is odds at close

---

The accuracy of closing line value is sport and market dependent. Often ante post markets basically at close will give you a good indicator as to where you are with your bet. Big line movements across the industry can stem from a few guys and they are not always right. The Efficient market Hypothesis is just that - theoretical - EMH may not be as sound as you might think.

CLV and Collin Morikawa at the Open Championship

At the Open Championship in 2021, Collin Morikawa drifted to 33s from 25/28s in the week, and he was 40.00+ on the betting exchanges. He won fairly easily. Why did he drift? Morikawa wasn't getting a lot of love that week. In fact, he was quite unfancied, and the narrative was links golf didn't suit. That's not false but it turned out there was next to no wind at Royal ST. Georges that week and that course can be played "through the air" American style in benign conditions. So, this would have been a great bet that offered significantly negative CLV but very high EV. This happens a lot in higher odds multi-field events where not many know the true odds. I'd advocate waiting until late in the market to catch some drifts in odds on Wednesdays in golf outrights. The more efficient markets are generally the lower odds two- or three-way markets that have much more liquidity behind them.

Handicapping is the number one skill in betting. Anyone who says it isn't, can't handicap. Closing Line Value has emerged as an alternative way to calculate and record a perceived longer-term edge and it's mainly used by "Steam Chasers" - also known as the top-down approach in the US. Again, it's not a new thing - it's been going on for many years in Europe since the emergence of odds comparison grids and Betfair.

Closing Line Value has its merits as an alternative way to track performance or as a backup but building a sample and recording your return on investment will still always be the number one indicator of skill in betting. Work out your expected value before all your bets and see how closely your return-on-investment percentage correlates to it over the longer term. In general, the better you are at handicapping (the more accurate you are at odds compiling), the smaller the sample you will need to show your true skill.

This is true so long as the variables you are weighting and the parameters you are using remain consistent. "Uncertainty" can often be quantified to a degree. If you are working with longer odds markets, it will take more time to even out the variance.

Bryan Nicholson
@NicsPicks   ...

Who is the better bettor after 20,000 bets ? The guy with:

10% ROI, matching pred.EV	33.2%
guy w 5% ROI but 15% CLV	18%
see results	48.8%

"Of course, the big CLV advocates are mostly steam chasers so they've no real accurate benchmark as to what the correct price should be beforehand. Therefore, the CLV truthers can be biased in assuming market efficiency"

You want to be on the right side of CLV on average over the long term in most markets, but CLV does not directly correlate to EV, it literally can't. After building a large sample portfolio of bets, if your actual return on investment (ROI) equates to your predicted EV that's the best benchmark.

This is true for me. If I had been measuring closing line value, overall, there wouldn't have been too much of it in the markets I exploit - mainly large field markets and prop markets. We want to be contrary to the market but that's not saying our prices *will actually be* too often.

The efficient market hypothesis in lesser, obscure, or higher odds markets is a fallacy. This statement is based on experience and years of empirical evidence. If your substantial return on investment percentage does indeed correlate to your expected value over a sample of tens of thousands of bets recorded, this is a true measure of skill and performance in sports betting.

Where is CLV a good benchmark?

Horse racing close to the time or a big Saturday football match will be a lot more accurate than golf outrights at close for example. Higher liquidity Pickems will be more accurate than longer odds markets, especially ones that change as much as golf. Spreads and Moneyline bets on the big US sports and two-way markets are usually pretty efficient.

This is not always the case though as we saw earlier when referring to Burnley vs Brighton and Everton vs Arsenal where usually the odds should be accurate. Don't just assume because there are some big players or syndicates controlling certain market lines that they are always right.

In fact, we should relish this. In golf right now there are some big steams on certain players throughout the week. These steams are dictated by certain sites with big influence and quite often the players fancied by the models are rubbish bets.

Efficient Market Hypothesis (EMH)

It has been empirically proven by the likes of Warren Buffett, but the "academics" will still oppose the theory of market IN-efficiency owing to the laws of probability and claim anyone beating the markets is down to luck or small sample size. These might be people who struggle to grasp small data and conditional probability.

The fallacy of market efficiency

The problem is back testing markets and results might average out to show efficiency but if you take all the markets or runners in a vacuum, many will be off by quite a bit. There's an argument around now about tipsters/handicappers and the above concept of closing line value and about CLV being a good benchmark to measure their success. Here's why that may not really be the case:

1. Markets are not as efficient as thought
2. The best handicappers are factoring in things the markets are not
3. The best bettors will be against the crowd often

This leads to low CLV and renders closing line value largely ineffective. As already alluded to, the true way of measuring success or skill as a bettor or handicapper is to track how close your actual ROI% correlates with your perceived (before the bets) expected value over a decent sample. The sample doesn't have to be that large contrary to what you may hear. Uncertainty can be estimated efficiently by real betting experts. This is also why P-values are not really that important in sports betting for more serious skilled bettors. We can refer to the Marco Blume and Pinnacle section.

Hakim Ziyech Example

This is the perfect example of extreme market inefficiency and it's a bet I had nothing to do with. This game was Chelsea at home to Villa in the league cup. A few days later at home to Man City in the league Ziyech was priced at 13/2, yes 13/2 with the same firm for 2x

Single

Chelsea v Aston Villa - #OddsOnThat - Shots On Target Specials

W   **Hakim Ziyech 1 or more right footed shots on   175/1
target & 1 or more left footed shots on target**

Stake: £2.00

Returns: £352.00

Boom! You have won £153.00

Single

Chelsea v Aston Villa - #OddsOnThat - Shots On Target Specials

W   **Hakim Ziyech 2 or more shots on target from   50/1
outside the box**

Stake: £3.00

Returns: £153.00

shots on target outside the box, versus his previous price of 50/1. And to think you usually get bigger prices vs better teams as well. It was a similar story with Leander Dendoncker who was priced at 250/1 for two headers on target in Wolves league cup game.

Some guys on Twitter got a huge payout doubling these two Ziyech and Dendoncker bets. There was a real opportunity to take advantage of these markets in football season 21/22 given the data from the Covid hit no fans season before.

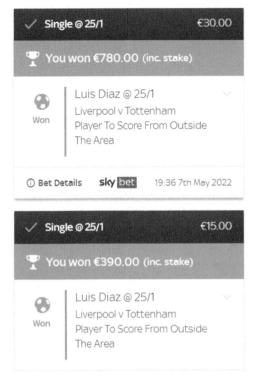

Luis Diaz was starting to shoot more and more from outside the box and look really dangerous in the process. Yet his 'to score outside box' price was going up and up as the data showed he hadn't yet done it for Liverpool. So much so, that the prime opportunity came along with Liverpool at home to Tottenham. Diaz was out to 25/1 with two books. Bang. Players' prices will ebb and flow in prop markets such as these based on their recent stats.

I expect Diaz to be regularly priced up at half these odds for much of season 2023. We could really take advantage of these types of bets throughout the 2022 footy season as they were being mispriced due to skewed data hanging around from the season before. In the FA Cup final, Liverpool vs Chelsea just one week later than this bet. Diaz continued to fly under the radar.

A certain sportsbook had him priced at 28/1 to score from outside the box versus Chelsea. He didn't quite manage it. In the game he literally had three great attempts from just outside the area, all very close - two of which grazed the post with the keeper in no man's land. If you think of it, 28/1 would almost break you even for the whole season if he did it just once. Twice, and your return on investment is over 50%. Pure madness. A full season for Diaz and he scores a handful of times from outside the box.

How do we determine true skill in sports betting?

We've touched on this topic in the book already. Is it about the size of our stakes? No. Several of the most gifted sports betting handicappers might be unknown and many are not big time stakers. This concept is just a myth - a fallacy people are taken by.

True skill in sports betting is measured not by the figure of money you make - it's all about how much you can beat the odds by. I'm not referring to closing line value, I'm referring to the odds obtained vs the actual true probabilities of all the bets you make over a big sample. Measuring this only comes through your long-term ROI%.

Your skill as a sports bettor comes down to how much percentage you can beat the books by, vig included. The closer your predicted expected value (EV) correlates to your actual return on Investment over the long run, and the higher your return on investment is, the bigger skill advantage you have over the bookmakers and the market.

Many of the top sports bettors will be sports handicappers, and more specifically the best sports handicappers will compile their own fair odds for the markets they are interested in which add to a true 100% book rather than a false bookmaker percentage with a margin added. The most skilled in the art of sports betting are people who study the sports and betting markets intrinsically to be able to quantify their edge.

Was Billy Walters a Handicapper?

The top-down approach or steam chasing is the other way to garner a real edge in sports betting. Many people that don't or can't originate odds will swear by the closing line as it is their only real measure of success or failure.

If we are an expert in compiling our own odds tissues, we won't be overly concerned with which way the line moves in a vacuum. Billy Walters is known as one of the best and biggest punters of all time in the Vegas rings. Walters himself wasn't what they called an originator. That means he didn't necessarily set his own odds.

Instead, he employed a network of highly skilled compilers and data scientists in their fields and cross matched their opinions. He picked out odds that were agreed upon and were lower in terms of true price than odds at books he could get action at. Walters had one specific employee he called his "Savant" - a genius in the data science department.

Still to this day some syndicates and bigger players operate in the same fashion by working together to get their most accurate odds and take on the bookmakers. There's more than one way to skin a cat and understanding how and why the markets are moving can mean you get on the right side repeatedly.

Walters' syndicate also manipulated markets to move lines and profit from the other side. He was an original master of what is known as the "head fake" in the US.

Odds boosts and enhanced odds

What you are getting with enhanced odds is essentially odds where the margin has been reduced or the fair price is now on offer. Sometimes at books this will offer some value and it can pay to shop around. Limits will be applied as they are there to entice action. We will see these offers based on the current narrative of the week such as a hot goal scorer to score first. I've seen some unscrupulous behaviour by certain firms in this department where they quote a price the day before then reduce the price on the day and then "boost" it back to the quote they had the night previous. That's shocking stuff in my book. There's a good example in the image below of one of these so-called "boosts" and I'm going to walk you through the unfairness behind it...

The boost is Webb Simpson apparently 4/7 to shoot birdie or better on either hole 1 or 2 of the Wyndham championship. 4/7 implies a 63% probability. Simpson had recorded 270 birdies on par 4s over 1258 attempts in his last two seasons. That equates to a birdie every 4.65 holes. If we adjust that slightly for the difficulty of the holes in question, we get around 1 in 4.5 or a 22% chance of making birdie on each hole. The probability of failing to make birdie or better on either hole then is (0.78 x 0.78) x 100 = .608, or 60%.

Was 4/7, Now EVENS! #golf

Simpson to birdie or better holes 1 or 2 in Round 1 of the Wyndham Championship

PRICE BOOST

Evens offered suggests 50% likelihood. Basically, our enhanced odds are offering us evens on a true 6/4 (40%) chance which is a negative expectation bet. The marketing makes it look to punters like they are getting good value. The reality is that some of these boosts can be very much what we call a negative expected value (-EV) bet, meaning we will lose over time backing this sort of thing.

We can refer back to the Virgil Van Dijk / Harry Kane examples of bad offerings as well.

Parlays and multiples

There is quite a bit of misconception going on around the betting world about multiples in sport. For the US bettors, a parlay is just what we call a "multiple" bet over here. An accumulator is when we roll several bets into one from what you might call a "parlay card". All have to win for a payout, and it's usually done for added excitement and in the hope of turning a few quid into a big payday. Bettors can assume wagering multiples is a bad strategy but that's assuming the edge is in the house's favour.

Are parlays the golden goose in betting or the quick way to the poor house?

Parlays are debated in the sports betting industry amongst more serious players as to their worth. Largely used by the recreational or "fun" gamblers chasing high pay-outs, parlay bets shouldn't necessarily be ignored by the elite player either. There is a margin or "hold" that's incorporated into the odds of each straight bet meaning that theoretically there's an edge in the favour of the bookmaker. This theoretical edge compounds for each selection or "leg" in the parlay, with the hold percentages being added together.

It can also work the other way though – if the edge in each bet is on your side you are increasing your own expected value (or EV). The downside is still there in terms of the variance as your returns will be less frequent in multiples bets. We can even add in some neutral expected value or maybe some slightly negative EV bets into the acca and still come out with a very big positive expectation bet, contrary to popular belief.

There are several different combinations of multiples. Permutation multiples are a great way to go for the Jackpot. A Round Robin is the US equivalent of this and in the UK, you might have heard of the famous "Trixie" or "Yankee" bet. These bets give ample opportunity to win and win big. They also allow you to reduce variance if you know how to play them correctly.

For example: I want to place a Yankee bet on four ballers to score in the weekend's footy fixture list. A Yankee bet consists of eleven bets, so your stake is multiplied by eleven. Let's say I do a €10 Yankee at €110. You are betting six doubles, four trebles and a fourfold acca in a Yankee. I target four players to score anytime at odds of at least 5/2 individually (+250). My return should two guys score is around 11/1 (this covers my outlay with one €10 double coming in).

If three players score, I'd get a return around 7x on my total outlay which would cover me for two months of weekends doing this bet. Should we strike 4/4 even once during the season, the yearly profits would be huge (about 40/1 on total outlay for the 4/4), so long as we keep the profit and loss (variance) graph steady with consistent returns from two and three guys coming up semi-regularly.

Ross McGowan Chapter

Yes, he gets his own chapter! Ross McGowan is a player I had in my notes as having an affinity with Cran Sur Sierre. These notes went back a long way and McGowan had been playing on different tours in the meantime. He had returned to the main stage with a win on the European Tour in the Italian Open in 2020 and the following year he got to tee it up at Cran again. I almost missed him in the field he was so far down the market.

McGowan was listed on my course fit manual which is a manual that flags players way in advance as ones to watch on specific courses given a strong fit, liking or previous history at them. He was 400/1 and 500/1 in places and ended up backed on the exchange before tee off at 1000.0. He was a tip during the week on Nicspicks.

Ross had returned to some sneaky form in the two events prior to the European Masters. If he didn't have this very recent upturn in form, I'd probably have left him out rather than back him on course fit or course history alone. As it was, it was an easy bet to put up, knowing what I knew, and that knowledge was not out there reflected in the market or prices at all. It generally wouldn't be anyway as a lot of it is subjective and this is an example of where the real big edges can be found in golf betting.

McGowan shot -2 in the first round. We were on board in the first-round leader market as well. This was quite a bit back from the lead on day one. He was off the planet in terms of being on anyone's radar, and on the Betfair exchange was being laid at 270/1 in the EW 1/5th ten places market. That's 54/1 on the top ten / or place side of that bet.

With an early tee time on the Friday which is usually worth around a stroke on average (but slightly more this week given the different scoring averages of the waves), McGowan still looked a very good betting proposition.

As it played out, he did put that low round in, shooting -6. Often what happens is that the late starters on the Friday who occupy most of the top positions on the board can stall in the afternoon when the wind is up and with faster and firmer conditions. McGowan was now -8 and just two shots back.

After round 3 he was right in it and trading around the 20.0 mark. On the final day he propelled himself into a two-shot lead on the back 9 and hit 2.40 on the exchange in running.

Pos		Country	Player Name	Today	Hole	Score	R1	R2	R3	R4
1	▲ 2	+	McGOWAN, Ross ⟳ODYSSEY	-4	9	-13	68	64	69	-
2	▲ 25		STENSON, Henrik ⟳ODYSSEY	-7	17	-11	71	64	71	-
	▲ 7		WIESBERGER, Bernd	-4	10	-11	67	67	69	-
4	▼ 3	( )	PARATORE, Renato ⟳ODYSSEY	PAR	8	-10	65	66	69	-
5	▲ 22	+	SLATTERY, Lee	-5	16	-9	70	67	69	-
	▲ 22	( )	MIGLIOZZI, Guido ⟳ODYSSEY	-5	16	-9	67	70	69	-
	▲ 16	+	ARMITAGE, Marcus ⟳ODYSSEY	-4	14	-9	63	73	69	-
	▲ 16	●	KAWAMURA, Masahiro	-4	13	-9	67	71	67	-
	▲ 4	●	SIEM, Marcel	-2	10	-9	66	68	69	-
	▲ 1		BURMESTER, Dean	-1	9	-9	64	65	73	-

Ross McGowan hit the front in Cran in the European Masters, trading at 2.40 from 1000.0

This would have been a brilliant win for us, not just in terms of big returns but in terms of the way the angle played out and getting money down on a more than decent betting proposition that not many people knew about. It didn't quite happen in the end, but he was either a lucrative trade or a huge-priced place at ¼ of 400/1.

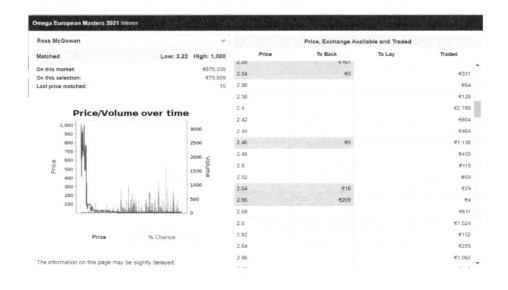

Lee Slattery example - a good golf trade

A bet I missed out on and wasn't very happy about was Lee Slattery at Albatross Golf Club for the Czech Masters in 2021. Slattery had pretty much everything I look for in a good golf bet in terms of course form, what I call hidden current form, and lots of value in a big price at 150/1 that I saw was being backed in on Wednesday pre-event. Slatts was what's renowned in the betting industry as a sea of blue on Oddschecker. This means he most definitely was not missed by some of the other shrewds, and the move was probably courtesy of some of the syndicates who play late.

Lee shot to the top of the leader board and on further inspection I noticed he had simmering form with two finishes around the 40th mark over the previous couple of weeks. This is a perfect example of how he will be overlooked in the pricing the following week as even I didn't notice him sneaking back into form and he hadn't been on my radar for quite a while. His immediate form included a closing 65 in Scotland just two weeks prior.

Slattery owned a t4 and a second-place finish in recent years at Albatross GC, demonstrating a real liking for the track.

This type of golf trend usually has some substance behind it. If you are modelling and or trading, you should look for opportunities like this to make money. To beat the market, you need to use the information that's not priced into the 150/1 odds, such as the "hidden form" he was carrying. This beats the bare data prices which include a sleeve of missed cuts entered into the algorithm. Lee would have been a good trade that week but didn't go on to challenge for the win. They often do.

Favourite Longshot Bias - Truth about odds, margin and the market

How would you operate if you were an independent bookmaker pricing up markets with the end game of maximising profit? The goal is to make punters make bad bets, and then balance the action as efficiently as you can so your margin / commission kicks in. In an ideal world you'd want risk- and stress-free markets with a properly balanced book.

Who are the punters likely to bet - the favourites or the longshots? In my direct experience, the guys in form are going to take the most money so why wouldn't the bookmakers try to take advantage of this? Their objective *should* be to add more margin to the front runners or most popular bets where the money is anticipated to flow.

The best way to get a balanced book is to weight (or shade) the margin / overround / hold towards the market selections that are going to attract the most money. It doesn't matter whether that's the front, middle or back of the market. Distributing the margin, depends on the market, the sports and the client base of the betting operator in question. It differs from market to market and depends on the variables in play for the event in question.

"We apply margin on a bell curve, meaning there is more margin added to the front of the market than the back" - Abelson Odds consult

---

This is a similar concept to sports betting in general - all markets are different. Margins can be applied algorithmically, guided by a bell curve, with the front end taking most % or they can be applied proportionally, equally or shaded. This bell curve method is the case for anytime goal scorer pricing in football at the big named "soft" sportsbooks in Europe, for example. Books need to guard against liabilities so in big EW markets, higher prices might have bigger margins incorporated.

There have been several academic papers and articles written, theorising the fave-longshot bias concept. These consist of back testing large, big data samples and using averages. This won't tell the whole story. It never does. We can refer again to the black box paradox. It doesn't add up and there is always a bias in these studies where a big data average can be massaged to fit the narrative. The studies done are largely from people who don't set odds and apply margins.

In terms of Expected Value for fave-longshot bias, more percentage baked into the favourites (shorter prices) doesn't necessarily mean more EV for the bookmaker or less for the punter. Small percentage differences in implied odds can equate to much larger EV / ROI %. It depends on the sport and the market how this works out.

"if 80/1 is your model price when handicapping but you know the rest of the market will be 45/50 then 55/1 would make sense, especially on a trendy, popular player who you know you will lay at that price" - Kambi

---

It's easy to confuse differences in implied probabilities (odds) percentages with expected value or return on investment %.

When serious bettors refer to their edge they are usually talking about their expected value in the market (EV), which equates to return on investment if calculated correctly. A small difference in implied percentage at long odds can equate to very high return on investment percentages.

Example

66 to 1 when turned into a percentage equates to 1.51%
50 to 1 implies 1.96% ....

This is a tiny difference of 0.45%.

So why is this worth betting? If we think of how casinos operate it's very similar in terms of small, fixed in built house percentage edges like this. Then they rely on volume - as many bets as possible over and over. Think of what physical casinos will do to keep players playing:

- Dim the lighting
- Cover the windows
- Free alcoholic beverages
- No clocks

If we place this type of bet (66/1 odds with true price of 50/1) many times over the course of the year we will realise our equity and this figure is a lot higher in EV percent, than the 0.45% in implied probability. We can plug the numbers into the expected value formula or use the betting tools EV calculator on Sharp sports Bettors...

$$(66*1.96) - (1*98.04) = 31.32\%$$

Expected value (EV) Calculator	
Stake	1
Probability of loss	98.04
Probability of win	1.96
Potential profit	66
EV ($)	31.32

This is an EV of 31.3% as we can see. I think a lot of people fail to realise how big these seemingly tiny edges (in terms of % differences in implied odds) turn into when relayed as ROI or expected value. Let's imagine a golf event where several players are priced up at 50s because the fair odds churned out by the model was 66s. But what if the true odds are 33s? You'd be looking at a long-term ROI of ~50%. This happens all the time in golf, on many players in each week/market and if we can get the volume of bets like this up over the course of the season we'll be in good shape long term.

Another concept experienced people get confused with is the overround/ juice/ hold in multi-way or big field markets. IE: big overrounds: 50% overround in a big field market is completely different to that type of margin in a ten or less runner field. 150% golf markets are not hard to beat - remember that the more runners, the less theoretical percentage margin each one has built in. The bigger the overround, the lesser the confidence level and the more room for error - that is the mantra you should adopt.

"What we do is very much a case-by-case basis, a lot of variables come into the decision" - Tristan Merlehan CEO of Topsport AU on applying the margin

---

I like to take every market and price it up on its own merit in a vacuum. I don't have any bias at all about going for shorter or longer prices. I weigh everything up against my 100% tissue prices and calculate the EV, leaving myself a bit of room for error.

Are favourites mispriced before the margin is applied?

We also must consider that the market might sometimes be off on the favourites. For example, the heuristical algorithms in place might weigh immediate form or big names / rankings too strongly and therefore the prices on the favourites are too short before the margin is even factored in. This is why I always refer to it as the "theoretical" margin or hold.

Harry Findlay gave a great example (subconsciously) of disregarding the favourite longshot bias in an interview. This is a man who actually understands the betting markets through living them empirically and betting them dry. He understands the markets nowadays and says that betting the short prices should be avoided. Findlay used to back the shorties - again, taking everything on its own merit. In this example he was referring to the dog racing and had an intuitive head for value where he'd back a very short priced odds-on dog that would still be way overpriced (in his mind). It worked.

Nowadays he says the short prices, or the favourites are generally way under-priced. Is this because of the margin or just mispriced races with favourites over valued? Perhaps it's a combination of both. Backing faves is a quick way to the poor house. Even if they were pushing out the prices on the faves then there's something fundamental wrong with the pricing algorithms as they are still too short implied probability wise, accidentally or on purpose.

To recap the fave-longshot bias -
it's a theory all about people perceiving there to be more value on the
bigger prices, but while the odds on the outsiders may look big, there is
actually quite a bit of a margin built into them. Whereas the favourites
are expected to be popular and you'd think the odds would be a little
tight, yet there isn't as much percentage built in as you'd think.

The above is the theory. It doesn't always work this way from my **direct** experience on both sides of the fence. In markets with two runners and low odds (moneyline, spreads, totals) - say a fight in the UFC, a darts match or even (but probably less so) a football match, maybe you'll see plenty of markets where there is an obvious protection barrier against the underdog and where the fave looked about fairly priced.

In sports and markets such as golf outrights, in terms of implied percentage, the front takes most of the book margin. If we look at the theoretical win percentage on the favourites in the golf markets and compare them to the percentages implied in the same market on Betfair we often see around 1.5% all the way up to 4% difference. Obviously the further down the market you go the less room there is to have big discrepancies in terms of implied percentages.

For example: any selection over 100/1 (of which there are many in golf markets) will have an implied win percentage of less than 1% and the difference between the book price and exchange price juice is then only a fraction of 1% implied probability. Remember we are talking about percentage differences here and not in relation to expected value. Longshot prices in the Each Way market will also need to be chopped to protect against the place payouts. This is similar in larger field horse races.

Even if the bookmaker / originator / trader thinks they are undercutting the price on the outsiders (or the favourites), they are not always right. They might make a selection 100/1, put him up at 50/1, but all the time said runner (given information unknown to the bookmaker), is actually a 33-40/1 shot. Most of the overround in terms of percentage in golf markets is implemented into the top ten in the betting. I've weighed up several golf match bets where the margin was in proportion vs my true odds and distributed on all sides of the win-draw-win in 3-balls.

We could really exploit these bets in 2021/22 after covid messed all the stats up. I personally know experienced traders that will differ in various markets in different sports depending on the brief. We can see proportional margin in the win-draw-win in golf matches, or the 'Outright' if we compare the books vs the Betfair price.

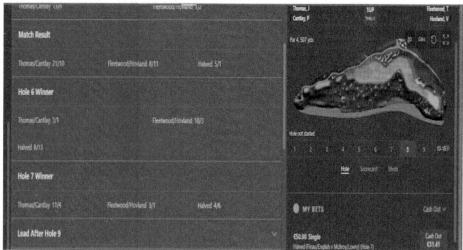

Caution: Take a look at some examples where the margin may have been implemented on the faves in the Ryder Cup match betting 2021.

 Bryan Nicholson @NicsPicks · 15h   •••

Cantlay / Thomas 11/4 (26.6%) Hovland Fleetwood 3/1 (25%) 4/6 (60%) half

111.6%

Extra margin on US side?

Hole 7 winner implies the above overround percentage - where is the margin built in?

As alluded to earlier, If I was a bookmaker pricing up events to make a profit, I'd want to be adding most of the margin in on the selections I anticipate the most money coming in on and adjusting accordingly from there. The most money was going to be coming in here in this match on the American side.

Most recreational bettors in my experience dive in on the shorter prices - I'm not sure where this theory is coming from that they like the longshots - they are not shrewd, and they want winners - that's my experience of recreational bettors in real life. The £5 pound punters at the bar watching the horses during the day, running in and out to the bookmakers next door each race, are mostly favourite backers with little regard for the price.

World Series of poker and Pokershares

In the final table of the World Series Of Poker in 2021 there were nine players left. Pro, **Koray Aldemir** was a significant favourite and had a decent chip lead. Many of the table were relatively unknown. It was clear that most of the money was coming in for Aldemir.

One big poker betting firm called Pokershares had Aldemir at just a shade over evens in the betting. Now, with my poker background specialising in Sit n' Gos and single table tournaments, I know the odds intrinsically. I had priced Aldemir at around 6/4 (40% likely to go on to win). Statistically it wasn't possible to do much better than this percentage against any calibre of player. The whole book was priced to around 110% which I thought was fair and I also noted I thought it was shrewd business on the market maker part to incorporate most of that margin on Aldemir, if this was indeed the case.

Fallon Sherrock was 4/6 in her ¼ final darts match. She was fave but was seeing the most money. I heard a podcast where Tom Brownlee discussed how he thought all the money was coming in for Fallon so despite being the favourite she had the most margin built in. I dare say he was right. Fallon was the big narrative, and everyone wanted to be in her corner. This type of thing happens all the time and dictates where the money flows. It would be bad business for bookmakers not to realise this and therefore shade the margin towards the favourite.

Brooks vs Bryson - the Match

Brooks Koepka and Bryson DeChambeau both came in at 10/11 in the betting in what looked a fair matchup. Also, in terms of money anticipated, half were in Bryson's camp and half were with Brooks in their online trolling battle. These prices were openers and after a while Byson was ⅘ and Brooks 1/1. It became apparent then that Bryson was more popular. Did they just price it wrong to begin with or did they implement more margin on DeChambeau when money began to flow?

WGC Matchplay at Austin CC

The WGC at Austin CC in 2022 had many match winners in the 6/4 to 7/4 range. On paper these looked like even enough matches. You would have made a big return backing these over the course of the tournament. The margin may have been implemented proportionally and if so, there was some serious mispricing across the industry.

Mispricing of favourites happens regularly in events like this. If the concept behind the prices is wrong, it tends to filter through the whole betting ecosystem and if there was indeed some shading of the margin it was on the side of the big names. In the third round of group games the guys with something to play for were overly short. The margin was baked into these players, not the "longshots" who had little to play for. No money was anticipated for the guys just playing for pride but as it turns out there was plenty of smart money on them. Pride should not be underrated in sport.

Masters 2022 Pricing at Circa Sports

Below is a golf betting market for the Masters where literally all the vig in theory is applied to the top twelve or so in the betting. There is big expected value on some of the guys outside that range. If money is anticipated to come on certain golfers, they will be targeted to add in more vig on them specifically, so how can the fave - longshot bias apply here?

Bryan Nicholson @NicsPicks · Mar 6 ···
Interesting Masters prices here at Circa. VS my prices and opinion the top 10 players are juiced up to the Maximus decimas meridius, while there's plenty of positive EV further down the market #favelongshotfallacy

ODDS TO WIN 2022 MASTERS TOURNAMENT		
J RAHM +840		
J SPIETH +1350		
J THOMAS +1550		
C MORIKAWA +1600		
V HOVLAND +1600		
P CANTLAY +1700		
D JOHNSON +1750		
B KOEPKA +1800		
R MCILROY +1850		
X SCHAUFFELE +1900		
B DECHAMBEAU +2800		
C SMITH +2800		
W ZALATORIS +2900		
H MATSUYAMA +3000		
S SCHEFFLER +3000		
D BERGER +4600		
S BURNS +5500		
T FINAU +6000		
J NIEMANN +6800		

In Play betting on the Ryder Cup

In play betting on the big events in golf can throw up some favourable betting markets, especially in props. A guy called Paulie on Twitter specialises in these bets and posted some plays on Twitter.

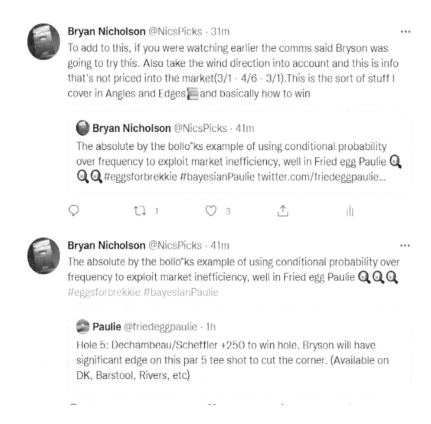

The above is an area that really can be exploited in the fourballs betting. In the example Bryson had such an advantage on a specific par 5 with a given wind direction that he could turn it into a par 4 by driving over a lake area. The others could not. This made the odds on Bryson's fourball winning the hole very tasty. You can see in the image above that the market was priced up all

 things equal. You'll rarely see this "conditional" stuff factored into the markets - it will be done on averages from general scoring data. Bryson did win this hole for his team with a tap-in eagle after flicking a wedge close.

"Well, I knew if it was a little downwind, I could take a unique line, and I luckily was able to have that wind today. It was 20-plus, and I said to myself, all right, I have to aim at the green, so I did. So, I just aimed at the green and bombs away" - Bryson deChambeau

We can also target strong par 3s and par 4's where the likelihood of making birdie is low, and there's plenty of juice to squeeze. We can usually find some betting opportunities. The probability of the elite pros making birdie on a par 4 is around 1 in 4.5 and on a par 3: one in five on average. If we consider par 4s around the 500-yard mark and par 3s around 200 yards and over, it's much lower than this. At the same time, the probability of **both** players making **bogey** (~one in four) is:

$(0.25*0.25) = 0.0625$

=> 0.0625 or 6.25% (or 15/1)

This shows birdie or better will be needed to win a hole in fourball. Most holes will be halved.

This image is portraying the average proximity on a tough hole from approach. Bear in mind the probability of holing out from 20' - 25' range on the PGA Tour is about 12%. Only one of these four approaches is within this zone. You can see below the type of odds offered on the half for each hole.

24/09/2021 23:02:21

Halved (DeChambeau/Scheffler v Rahm/Hatton) (Hole 17)   4/6

€50.00 Single

Stake €50.00   **Return €83.34**

Bet Details   >

24/09/2021 22:58:27

Halved (Thomas/Cantlay v Fleetwood/Hovland) (Hole 15)   10/11

€50.00 Single

Stake €50.00   **Return €95.46**

Bet Details   >

24/09/2021 22:45:08

Halved (Johnson/Schauffele v Casey/Wiesberger) (Hole 17)   4/6

€50.00 Single

Stake €50.00   **Return €83.34**

Bet Details   >

24/09/2021 22:43:47

Halved (Finau/English v McIlroy/Lowry) (Hole 15)   10/11

€50.00 Single

Stake €50.00   **Return €95.46**

Bet Details   >

We can shop around for lines and get anywhere from 4-6 to evens on these types of bets. That implies on average a win probability of 56-57% whereas I make the true win percentage of these bets somewhere between 70-75% on the tougher holes. In terms of EV that equates to around a 30% return on investment over time.

Patrik Cantlay answer on why the Europeans have such a strong record in the Ryder Cup

"So, I've read a few gin books. Let's see if I get it right. If you play enough gin hands a one or two percent difference in skill translates to almost an assured win over many, many, many hands of gin. But you could have a big difference between somebody, maybe a 60 to 40 percent skill level difference, and gin is still chancey enough to where you could play ten hands and lose six or seven of the hands than someone that's much worse than you skill-wise.

"Really there's only two — these matches are only played every two years, and golf is very chancey. So would it surprise you if the U.S. went on a similar run to what Europe has been on for the next 20 years. Wouldn't surprise me. You go to Vegas, and you play roulette, and the chances are 50/50 but skewed toward the house a little, it could hit red six times in a row, but that's not abnormal. You flip a quarter.

It would be weird if the quarter flipped tails, heads, tails, heads, tails, heads. Then you would think something trippy was going on.

"I try to take a very long-term view on things like that. Who knows? The captains are different every year. The players are different every year. The venues are different every year. The weather is different every year. You're really going to ask a question like that and think you're going to get the right answer? I don't have the answers to that"

Patrick Cantlay could have answered this question with one word - what he is unknowingly describing here is **variance**. What's most interesting to me though is the 1 -2% edge in Gin.

Consider that this is a similar percentage on average to the theoretical margin applied to each golfer in an outright market. Using course fit alone, if you have a strong predictive model or even better, a smart mind, and can target golfers with an actual high course fit rating, this variable is worth a fair bit more percentage wise than 2%, therefore really pushing the long-term edge in your favour. This is the way expected value works but I never thought of the course fit concept specifically like this until I saw Patrick's answer here.

Note: the pattern of the coin going head-tail-head-tail-head-tail would be no weirder than six heads or tails in a row, they are all the same probabilities.

Following this passage from Cantlay, the US smashed the Ryder Cup record by going 19-9 against the Europeans. It played out maybe as expected on paper but in my opinion, there were two things not given nearly as much weight as they should have been in terms of how the tournament went.

Firstly, the lack of European fans was huge - it must have been a terrible environment for the European golfers getting absolutely nothing when they holed out or won a hole, except some boos and abuse from a section of US bandits. The silence was eerie. The main variable though was once again **course fit**. The Straits was set up for the aggro bomber friendly player and every single US Player basically fit this profile. I said during that week that the US side essentially reversed the Ryder Cup at Paris National by "course fitting" the Euros into submission. This is what team Europe did to the US in France; only, the US were close to the same starting price (around 1.6) when the odds should have been the other way around in France, as I'd written in my 2018 preview.

Seven of the last eight Ryder Cups have now been won by the home side. Why? A lot of it is down to course set up - IE course fit and because the home team gets to decide how the track plays.

The absolute demolition by the home sides in the last two editions was largely down to course fit.

Some will argue that the sample is too small. I'll argue that sound reasoning and logical skills will win out in the betting markets over time - in small samples, and much of the uncertainty can be quantified.

An analogy

A 20 handicapper has a probability of shooting one birdie in fifty holes. Would you lay odds of 3/1 he has a birdie in his next round? His true odds are around 2/1 so no, you should be offering around 7/4 as the layer with a little bit of juice on your side.

Is it 50/1 to have a bird on each individual hole he tees it up? That's the lazy way of pricing, on averages. But no, it's conditional, based on the hole indexes. It might be 20, 50 and 100 to 1 true odds for the different sets of indexes: high, medium, low. We could theoretically exploit this by line shopping different bookies looking for the bigger price when we play on the higher index holes, and by doing this we can exploit even though the edge is on the layer side taking it round by round.

Risk Intelligence

There's a process called risk intelligence which is where some people might have the ability to process all variable information in their head like a computer and turn it into probabilities. It's done almost subconsciously as if empirical evidence from the past has been recorded and stored, and your brain is running multiple iterations to estimate probabilities. Some people can work out conditional probabilities like in the above example without using computers, models and data. Like in the logical-mathematical approach at the start of HBN, they already know the answer before they articulate it.

Risk intelligence is the ability to estimate probabilities accurately

The fundamental flaw in Averages

Collin Morikawa is renowned for his approach shots and iron play. What happens if he has a mediocre six months in that department and is ranked 75th for strokes gained approach? Does this make him an average iron player relative to his peers? Some people based on a modelling approach alone would come to the *yes* conclusion. These people can be destroyed in the betting world. Golf variance is a very long-term game. We are literally not interested in stats that were derived from when a player was out of form when measuring true ability.

The true ability of a player will generally be somewhere around the mean of performance at their baseline and at their ceiling. It's our job to quantify this. For the nerds out there, we can use something called box plots. I prefer to use my brain. Anyone swearing by strokes gained stats from the official sites will be caught out in sports (golf) betting. All you're doing is using the same technique as the flawed odds compiling method you're trying to beat, and you're coming up with the same non-precise numbers.

I saw the below example on twitter where a guy wasn't understanding that shotlink uses a straight line from point A to point B. I thought it was a great analogy of what's wrong with betting markets and how the wrong conclusions can be drawn by not factoring in what goes on behind the scenes. That's how the market black box of averages works.

 Bryan Nicholson @NicsPicks · Mar 6   ···
This thread has a fine analogy with betting markets and what goes on behind the "black box".Shotlink shows a straight line between 2 points: where the shot started and where it finished. It doesnt show what went on for it to get from A to B. This is why bare data can fail in both

Mar

Bones described conversation between Billy Horschel and unnamed player in group in front as "very interesting" over whether Beau Hossler's ball crossed the penalty area. A shame there was no @NBCSports video shown of the shot or this very interesting conversation. @APBayHill

What happened here was that shot link showed a ball in the water (where it finished). There was a debate as to whether it crossed the hazard. Shot link would be inconclusive as it doesn't show the whole path of the ball before it came to rest.

First Round Leader in Golf

The first round leader market in golf is a prime example of a market handcuffed by the data models. For years this market was basically the outright odds imported which saw baby changes over a long period of time, until finally in 2019 the massive inefficiency was fixed. I personally destroyed this market for ten years, not in terms of huge staking profits but in terms of return on investment percentage. Obviously with markets such as this (which a lot of firms referred to as specials markets), limits and factoring and even banning will be quick enough to come into play.

The process was simply to target three figure guys out early with strong course fit/progressive form who I knew were aggressive low scorers. It was like playing a hugely mispriced and plus EV lottery. Back a group of these guys in each tournament each way and keep variance low throughout the season with the place payouts. You'd only need a handful of winners for big profit.

In professional golf the difference between 18 holes and 72 holes is huge. I'd have thought this was just logical and obvious to supposed experts trading it. Without the data to back it up though it didn't seem to be the case. The odds in the first round leader market should be a much narrower range. As more holes are played the better players will tend to come to the fore. This is also why extra places are so important in golf betting. Favourites were massively under-priced in the FRL market and many underdogs were hugely overpriced. We could see 150/1 shots that were just as likely as 50/1 shots to be amongst the front runners after round one if we knew what variables to look out for - course fit and tee times being the number one and two. On average an early tee time in golf on the Thursday or Friday is worth almost a full stroke.

One stroke is huge in this market - it eliminates a large proportion of the afternoon starters given the median score is one worse. This is an average and it depends on actual weather conditions on the week in question. Again - it's all conditional!

Over time this market became much more popular, and more data was being recorded. The problem was there were no first round market originators back in the day. Then the market on Betfair started to become more and more liquid, leading to the corporate sportsbooks' prices becoming more efficient. I'm not sure whether there are now specialists supplying the odds for this market to the main bookmakers, or how much copying is going on. One thing is for sure the Betfair market has a big part to play in shaping more accurate numbers these days. The edge now in the first round leader market is nowhere near where it used to be but being more selective there are still opportunities.

Hole in one probabilities in Golf Betting

Below is the distribution of hole in ones or aces during the 2021 golf betting season on the PGA Tour and DP World Tour. I recorded circa 136,000 par three shots or attempts. All of these won't have been at the pin, but we don't want to over complicate things and I dare say plenty of actual hole in ones won't have been aimed at the pin in any case. We covered around eighty tournaments overall and saw 66 aces. Added to the previous year, we have around 120 aces recorded from around 230,000 par three attempts in total across the DP World Tour (European Tour) and PGA Tour.

The simple heuristics of the maths answer gives you the probability or odds of an elite pro golfer hitting a hole in one as around 1900 to 1 from one attempt. This is how bookmakers would price it up, but it's not as simple as that in real life and we can easily exploit this. The real answer is that it depends, each and every week. It's conditional, as are most betting markets. It's all about the difficulty of the par three hole in question and the pin placement. We can even factor in the weather if we want extremely accurate probabilities.

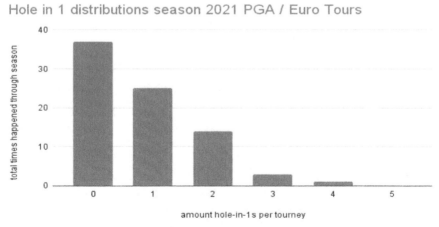

Hole in 1 distributions season 2021 PGA / Euro Tours

Distribution of hole in ones across the PGA and European Tour in 2021

It's around 10,000 to 1 on average for a hole in one to be recorded across amateur golf. These are the figures from the World Handicap System (WHS). In elite pro golf it can be as low as 200/1 and as high as 5,000 to 1 plus, for an ace, depending on the par three hole in question - it differs that much. Think the 16th at Augusta with the pin down the back bottom left of the hill, vs a par three with the flag on a plateau over 220 yards long.

The Hole in one Gang

The hole in one gang was a group of golf bettors back in the day who truly understood probability. Many bookmakers did not. These were the days of betting when there was no online content or exchanges. It was each to their own prices and all sorts of odds were being quoted for a hole in one in professional golf tournaments - from 7/4 to 100/1! The hole in one gang exploited that by travelling around individual bookmakers across England and placing all the multiple bets they were allowed. Long story short - they made a small fortune. To this day people are still underestimating the likelihood of this sort of thing.

Phoenix Open - The 16th hole at TPC Scottsdale

There have been eleven holes in one recorded in thirty-five years on number sixteen at the Phoenix Open at TPC Scottsdale. That equates to a hole in one every 1400 attempts or so there on average. Bear in mind pin placement can have a huge impact on these odds. Six from eleven of these aces came on the Saturday of the events when the pin is at the front left of the green and it plays at around 120 yards to wedge distance. No coincidence here. 2022 saw just the second time two aces on sixteen in the same week were recorded.

What odds Ortiz?

Carlos Ortiz was one of the guys who holed out for an ace on number sixteen that week. If we use the heuristics figures of 1400 to 1 to do this and check the stats on eagles recorded at seventeen in the week (6 in 390 or so attempts), then multiply these probabilities together, that would have made him around 90,000 to 1 (himself) to go 1-2 (ace/eagle) when standing on the tee box at number sixteen. He was around 65/1 to make eagle alone at seventeen which does seem a little big.

Let's get psychological...

The Clustering illusion and streaks in Sports

The clustering illusion is described as the tendency to erroneously consider the inevitable "streaks" or "clusters" arising in small samples from *random* distributions to be non-random. I'm not sure where the clustering illusion theory came from originally but if they think streaks in sports are all random, I'd like a bookies full of them. They would be strongly mistaken.

The great thing for shrewd sports bettors is that prices are indeed set with this concept in mind, especially prop betting markets and specials, often "enhanced". A smallish sample will often disregard streaks to chance, and it wouldn't work any other way. The bookmaker only has to beat the collective on the averages and will do that, but each market taken in a vacuum is a separate entity in itself.

The truth is that in sports, many streaks are not random at all. They are more often than not largely or at least loosely down to two main variables (a whole lot of other factors can apply too): **form and confidence**, which correlate to each other.

An example is a striker scoring goals will build confidence, getting into better positions and will make the runs into the box and finish with aplomb. Or a midfielder like Naby Keita did this for Liverpool in 2022 when he scored versus Atletico, and then he scored twice in two running games versus Man UTD.

Coincidence? No, he was playing a more forward role and you could see when he scored his first goal that he was full of confidence and making forward runs and shooting, like he wasn't previously doing.

This concept might be referred to as being like the **Hot Hand Fallacy** but it's not a fallacy at all in sports betting.

> The "hot hand" is a phenomenon, previously considered a cognitive social bias, that a person who experiences a successful outcome has a greater chance of success in further attempts

-        *wiki*

A "hot hand" in basketball may stem from a player making three consecutive shots. It's argued we may believe he has a greater chance of making the fourth than is likely, but I'd argue back maybe the player has a handle on the trajectory of the shot, and extra confidence leads to these streaks. That's very true in these circumstances, unlike the Gamblers / Monte Carlo Fallacy that has no "conditional" element to it, but it's a different ball game when it comes to sport if you excuse the pun!

If you hit five blacks in a row in roulette, the probability of either red or black on the next spin does not change. The Monte Carlo fallacy stems from roulette players thinking the red was "due" after a string of blacks came up, and they did their conkers! If I saw this, if anything, I'd be smashing black, black, black thinking something dirty was going on! I *have* seen a run of around twenty of one colour in roulette. At the casino in Monte Carlo that day, it didn't revert to red until spin number 27.

Consider this... A golfer for the year might spend half his season in average form which will be around his baseline performance. His weekly price won't deviate too much from this average over the season. He might then spend ¼ of the season out of form and ¼ in top form. Out of the three months he spends in top form he might have two spells (streaks) of three or four weeks where he records most of his best results. This is common if you look up historical data of players on the main golf tours. Our job as sports bettors is to identify when these streaks look on the horizon and then strike vs bookmaker prices that will be still centred around that baseline, as traders are using a more frequentist approach to pricing. During the ¼ of the year he's in form, his prices should be maybe half his baseline, and the ¼ he's out of form maybe they should be 2x his baseline. If we back him at 50s vs a true price of 25s and lay him at 50s vs a fair price of 100s in these different spells where we have identified the streaks, we will theoretically make a lot of money.

"a golfer earns most of his money for the year in just a few weeks/ couple of tournaments" - Paul McGinley

High level betting is all about psychological warfare and applying conditional probability to events to calculate truer probabilities than what gaussian distribution or the frequentist maths approach will output - what the algos do to price up. The best way to realise this edge is to put in the 10,000 hours watching and analysing empirically.

The nerdier among us can use the advanced modelling approach but I always wonder how they can bet confidently vs prices they can't really quantify in their own head. A mix of the two would be great! There is also option three which is the top-down steam chasing approach. The other side of the battle is all about risk management and the fundamental mathematics side of things that we as bettors *actually* need, as opposed to the in-house traders who are the opposite (they need all the formulaic maths skills and not necessarily the betting smarts). Luckily enough I also have you covered on this front in my third book on the *maths of sports betting*!

> *Dunning-Kruger effect, in psychology, is a cognitive bias whereby people with limited knowledge or competence in a given intellectual or social domain greatly overestimate their own knowledge or competence in that domain relative to objective criteria or to the performance of their peers or of people in general. Whereas people with high ability or skill level at a task may underestimate their own ability*

- wiki

This is twitter all over. So many people are so bullishly wrong. If people are naturally gifted in a domain or have a specific intelligence (like risk intelligence) that not many people have, it comes automatically and it's easy for them, so it makes sense that they may underestimate their abilities. The ones who overestimate their abilities just can't see what they are missing and that's where the confidence comes from. This is where the market efficiency fallacy comes from - mass cognitive biases.

"The problem with the world is that the intelligent people are full of doubts, while the stupid ones are full of confidence"

- Charles Bukowski

Cognitive biases in Sports Betting

I've seen it all. I watched people for months, even years, poo poo the likes of Tony Finau and Patrick Cantlay repeatedly, only to see the very same guys jumping on the bandwagon when Finau and Cantlay came good. It was like they almost convinced themselves they hadn't been calling him a choker etc. Finau got that win in a big event against a world class field overcoming Jon Rahm down the stretch. Cantlay won three or four times and bagged the FedEx Cup showing those massive balls of steel in a mad playoff with Bryson. Suddenly, some past performances (which was just variance) were forgotten.

What is the House Money Effect?

The House Money Effect is described as a theory used to explain the tendency of investors to take on greater risk when reinvesting profit earned through investing than they would when investing their savings or wages. "People will often think about investment income as separate from the money they earned in other ways, which distorts their mental accounting."
Because that money is incorrectly considered somehow "extra" or "separate" from money earned in other ways, investors will invest it with a much higher risk tolerance than they would otherwise, thereby skewing their investment decisions.

The House Money Effect states that:

> The house money effect, which Thaler and Johnson (1990) first propose and document based on experimental evidence, refers to a pattern whereby people tend to take on increased risk subsequent to a successful investment experience. That is, prior gains lead to greater risk taking in subsequent periods

- *Investopedia*

Can starting fast be a recipe for disaster?

The House Money Effect is definitely a thing, even for me to a degree, and is what I refer to as a "freeroll". It is another psychological affliction that if not understood and controlled can have detrimental results on a bettor. I've come across rich poker players or NFT crypto guys essentially leading an ego based existence on social media where they think buying worthless sh!te gives them some status.

This is generally money they've accrued through other forms of gambling - mainly bitcoin / crypto, and it seems like they don't even see it as real money. Some "investors" try to exploit this attitude so you may see some "smarties" in there doing their thing. Groups and individuals are minting these NFTs or dropping PFPs and many of these projects came out to take advantage of the rich Bitcoiners buying essentially junk.

NFT aficionados were spending multiple thousands of pounds on videos that were available for all to download online or buying jpegs of rocks and "Cryptopunks". It must be said that some shrewder operators were buying only with the intention of selling higher. Anyone doing this sort of thing must have a distorted view of money, and indeed much of their wealth was accrued through the gambling medium and exists (in their heads) only in the virtual wallet world.

An important lesson in staking and Discipline

You should have a separate betting bank to your life roll. While it's extremely important not to stake above your comfort level for a multitude of reasons, including state of mind, wealth, and variance, it's equally important not to stake too low versus your net worth and here's why:

Have you ever played the play money games in poker or in some sort of online bet simulator or social app vs your friends? If so, think back to your performance. How efficiently did you do things compared to how you would have done if you had real skin in the game?

When I was younger and rising through the online poker ranks there were plenty of tournament freerolls offered as part of bonuses, or you could register in some play money tournaments if you were a newbie and wanted to learn and experience the game. These freerolls were not of much interest to me. The prize pools were not great and the fields were deep, so it wasn't worth putting my time into.

So how did I perform?

When entering one of these tournaments, (bear in mind it was similar to being registered for some lower than normal stakes tournaments) on average, my performance was well below par. Many things were done that I wouldn't do if it was more important to me and several plays were made that were wrong, but I just didn't care. It's very similar in sports betting when you might have a few bets "for fun" in certain games or events. The exact same concept applies in betting on sport. If having a fun bet, it would never be a large one in proportion to my bankroll.

During the covid period through sheer boredom I was knowingly making some minus EV plays on the footy games.

Even if you are betting seriously, it can be hard to eliminate these types of recreational bets from your portfolio, especially if you are someone like me who enjoys the buzz of watching the games play out with a bit of money on them. This is known as **discipline** and it's the one area of the game where I've what you'd call a substantial weakness.

There are many factors that contribute to indiscipline including:

- Set up
- Emotional conditioning, frustration and tilt control
- Sleep, fitness and energy levels
- Boredom
- Gambling problem
- Lack of record keeping

I went through a period of not feeling too well and was very tired and quite bored with it all. All the fundamental leaks gradually came into my betting including over staking and chasing. Not really caring at that stage, it was still an eye opener to see just how easy it is to lose money, despite being highly skilled in picking strong value bets.

The fundamentals are so important. This period kind of coincided with doing a lot of trials and adapting, looking to find where my big edges still were and seeing if I could add any new ones to the repertoire. This takes time - especially in golf where there are only around 80-100 tournaments a year, which is quite a small sample. Disillusionment set in for an extended period and burn out will happen to anyone if you are not doing the right things and managing your life and health well.

Poker for me on and off was a very similar experience. Making plays like opening 8h9h out of position or three or four betting that kind of hand in position too often are all leaks that can easily slip into your game. It can be a bit of an ego thing as well, especially if you have an aggressive type gambling personality.

Sometimes it's hard to spot the fundamental flaws leaking back into your performance and it's detrimental to your bottom line. I was a 'sucker for value' you might say, and could easily be over aggressive, making too many plays/bets on anything seen as a bit of value. Suited connectors in poker would be akin to a 12/1 shot you think should be 10s and you're hammering away with little regard for variance or even the fact that they may not actually be a play - you could be wrong. It's sometimes smart to wait for better opportunities and higher expected value plays to eliminate uncertainty and bad bets.

It's also very important to keep records to see every area you are doing well (and not well) in. The more detailed record keeping you do the quicker you will spot trends showing you where your edge might be increasing or decreasing.

If you keep a spreadsheet detailing all your results it's surprising how easy this is, and what shows up. Make sure you get all the fundamentals correct before looking to bet seriously or you're fighting a losing battle from day one.

Keep your bet and stake sizings in check and bet within your means. Have a separate bankroll for betting and poker or whatever form of gambling you partake in. Study all the staking systems and find something that suits. Level staking is a good place to start and is the next best to the Kelly Criterion (or variant of) staking.

Introduction to Probability Theory

Book no. 3 in my trilogy will cover all the fundamental maths and go into detail about probability theory and conditional probability. This chapter is an introductory chapter on probability and its application in sports betting. Don't run before you can walk....

> *Probability is a mathematical term for the likelihood that something will occur. It is the ability to understand and estimate the possibility of a different combination of outcomes*

Probabilistic thinking is using a combination of logic and maths to estimate the likelihood of any event occurring from a percentage perspective. We can use a process known as statistical inference over small samples to estimate the parameters of what is known as a population (specific sample). This is what I've been applying versus the betting markets and poker tables for the best part of twenty years. The sports betting markets are formed with a more frequentist approach to probability based on long term averages (mean, over median), and with the use of what I'd describe as mathematical heuristics - universal formulae that do an efficient but not great job of pricing up, overall.

We can pick the markets apart individually. If you look at my course fit model in golf, it's all about using my best estimates of key parameters. **We call this empirical inference.**

There are three main types or areas of probability in the real world:

- Theoretical probability / belief (Bayesian)
- Experimental Probability / data (Frequentist)
- **Conditional Probability /axiomatic probability (logical)**

Odds, models and algorithms are based around frequentist statistics. Applying conditional or situational probability is how we can beat them. We often hear frequentists (maths guys) say there's no "proof" or "evidence" as their argument but why would we need mathematical evidence for common sense? Is the grass green or do we need to count 10,000 blades to be sure?

This is just over complicating sports betting, which is all about understanding, inherently, the more trivial maths and then it's about applying logic and common sense to the markets and numbers to find angles and edges. It's not about applying more advanced maths to fundamental concepts. That's how odds are set across the industry - we want to beat these odds, not fight fire with fire.

Bayesian Inference

Bayesian Inference is an amalgamation of logical-mathematical reasoning, subjective probability and qualitative analysis. The term "Bayesian" wasn't actually around when I studied probability - back then it was known as the "Inverse". Someone said to me recently that the new kids just have fancy names for what we do intuitively. This is indeed the case in some areas and several old sports betting concepts now have been rehashed under new names and guises. CLV for example, or "Line shopping".

Bayesian inference is a concept that stems from the Bayes Theorem, formulated by Thomas Bayes, which is a theory about conditional probability. I use this (largely intuitively) and apply it when looking for an edge in the betting markets. Small data vs big data. I keep talking about the markets being made based on big data and long-term averages. We can unlock this using conditional probability - studying those mini clusters within the big data and finding patterns with true signal.

What is the Bayes Theorem? It's a formula used to estimate conditional probabilities.

$$P(A \mid B) = P(B \mid A) * P(A) \; / \; P(B)$$

The Bayes theorem is a formula for conditional probability which reads: the probability of A given B equals probability of B given A multiplied by probability of A, divided by the probability of B.

How can we apply it in betting? When you look at the betting markets, whether they are compiled in house, at a consultancy or even if it's just the market formed on the exchanges by a combination of the syndicates, consultancies or big players, it doesn't matter - the prices you see especially earlier on, rather than towards close, will be largely based around "big data".

"Big data contains greater variety in larger volumes and with more velocity. Put simply, big data is larger, more complex data sets, especially from new data sources" – wiki

I'm going to use a very good analogy to demonstrate inefficiencies in frequentist probabilities when pricing markets and how we, being selective, can apply conditional probability to get more accurate estimates and therefore seek out big value in the sports betting markets.

Car park analogy

If you record the number of cars parked in a space over the whole day, multiply that figure over a week and a month and a year, then compare it to the spaces available, and take an average, you are going to get a certain ratio.
Will your percentage chance of getting a free space be the same at all times of the day on each random day? No. If bookmakers were pricing this up, they usually won't factor the different times of day in (the conditional). It's the very same algorithm in betting markets, just using the 'big data' average. Heuristics.

The probability of attaining a parking spot can be vastly different depending on the time of day - morning, lunch, weekend, rush hour etc. This is the logic I apply to beating the markets and the margin. People refer to the wisdom of the crowd and exchange markets being very efficient at closing if they are liquid but it's not always the case due to what I have said above - the underlying concepts of these markets are built from. This will never really change at bookmakers - they basically don't have the time, the need or the manpower to base the odds on Bayesian inference which includes the situational factors. Not many people are that smart anyway, and you'd need to pay to get them.

You can't just lump everyone (all the cars and spaces and times) into the same population. It doesn't work that way. People are not machines, and they perform differently at various times, just like the car park will be more and less busy at certain times. We can use the Bayes Theorem to estimate our **true** chances of getting a car parking space at our **specific** time.

Conditional probability is defined as a measure of the probability of an event happening given that another event by, presumption or evidence, that affects the percentages has occurred

---

We can see some more examples of applying this concept to sports betting…

To use some more gambling analogies

What's the probability of being dealt a King in Holdem? There are four Kings in a deck of 52 cards. Each player is dealt two cards so:

4/52 * 2 = 2/13 or 0.154 (15.4%) (two in 13 holdings)

What if we could see some cards - does this conditional change the probabilities? Yes. When we are working out odds in poker it's about our "outs" in terms of unseen cards. Let's say there were four opponents with cards turned up on the table and another four opponents who mucked their cards. One opponent was holding a King. The maths would now be:

$3/36 * 2 = 0.166$ or 16.6% probable as opposed to 0.154 (15.4%)

You now have just three chances of being dealt a King and sixteen of the 52 cards are excluded from the deck so there's 36 left to pick from. You have two cards to be dealt to you.

In golf betting, the probabilities change if for example the track is so long that half the field is at a significant disadvantage, or if betting the top twenty market the players most likely are the ones in current form, not necessarily the best players. You must weigh it all up. It's no use backing Bubba Watson for a top twenty if he's driving it off the planet and playing army golf at a course with big trouble left and right off the tee.

Max Homa and Tony Finau were in a playoff at Riviera. They were playing the drivable short par 4 10th hole and Max looked like he put it behind a tree. The camera angle quickly showed that the tree was not really going to hamper his chip shot, yet with Tony being close enough for an eagle chance the market had backed him into 1.10. This was some opportunity for the shrewdest of golf punters. The likelihood of Homa getting up and down was somewhere around 70% and it was the same for Finau missing. Therefore, it was around evens for the playoff being extended yet Big Tony could be laid at 1.10. I call this the anti-green lumber fallacy! This is where lack of knowledge in playing the sport itself can let you down, regardless of expertise in the markets. We can refer to the **Brighton example** in the efficient market hypothesis section where their expected goals were just wrong because the 'conditional' probability says that Brighton had bad strikers against the average. These are all examples of where the "conditional" isn't being considered and therefore the odds will be off.

Matched betting and Exchange Hedging

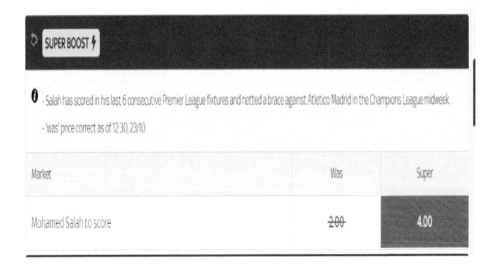

An interesting situation developed on the exchange the day of Liverpool's visit to Manchester UTD in the 2021/22 season. What happened was Sky Bet offered a super boost of Mo Salah to score anytime at 3/1. Now this, despite limits, in such a big match will cause all sorts of hedging opportunities for traders with prices drifting out on the exchange.

Matched bettors will have a field day as well and had a big part to play here, so it led to about 40k in liquidity out of 42k (this is total anytime scorer market still four hours before the game). It was posted on twitter to instigate price movement then the price contracted in towards fair (reverse line movement of sorts) creating lots of trading volatility.

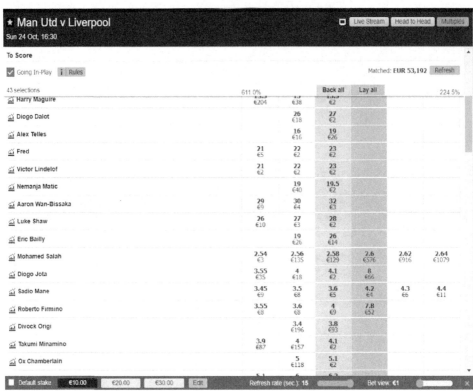

Most of the liquidity in this market was through Mo Salah due to his superboost price on SB

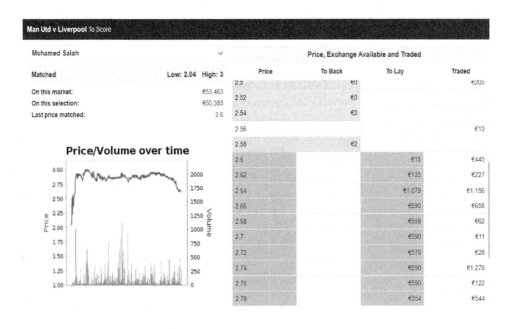

This situation brought me back to the argument about hedging vs letting bets ride for maximum expected value. What people fail to understand here is that you're not actually making a -EV bet by hedging if your plan in the first place was to turn your bet into a trade at certain fixed odds (allowing for the small amount of EV you would be giving up). It's like making a winning bet on the exchange knowing you're going to pay a small commission. If you predict these odds would be hit at a rate giving you value for a trade, it's an overall trade with positive expectation. The lower the odds get in running, the closer to fair they become anyway. If you trade out at fair odds it makes no difference in the long run, it's the same expected value.

Matched betting is more of a newer concept akin to bonus whoring. It involves opening many new sports betting accounts to take advantage of sign up offers and free bets. You simply use the exchange to hedge against your free bets at close to neutral EV to make them risk free and meet rollover requirements to turn the free bets into cash.

Poker and DFS Corner - A Sports Betting Analogy

We mentioned in the preface of the book that high level poker is the very same as sports betting in terms of probability, maths and statistics, and applying conditional probability to every situation. It's about knowing the odds, percentages and best positive expected value plays, game theory (GTO) wise, and then adjusting for the situation. There's no better primer than top level poker to get you accustomed to variance and simulating what can happen over the long run-in sports betting.

I want to talk specifically about what happened in the poker boom and the similarities with what is happening in the sports betting, data-oriented era. If you don't play poker regularly to a high standard, you'll be unaware of the correlation, but this is a very important chapter in terms of understanding **sports betting**. The betting models you keep hearing sports bettors talk about these days are essentially the poker *Solver* equivalents. Here's the catch: both concepts and softwares are severely limited.

My Poker Background

My journey in poker began in my early twenties playing limit Hold'em and going through the bonuses, multi-tabling online. This is the game type I played while learning all about position, ranges, and all the odds and percentages - basically the mathematical side of the game. I moved on and found my niche in Single Table Tournaments (STTs) and Sit N' Gos playing predominantly six-seater STTs. At my peak I had a return on investment in the region of 20% (like sports betting) at low to mid stakes in this format and was tracking in the top 1% of online players in these games. A lot of the names you see in poker nowadays were part of my player pool at that stage. I've since gone on to play live poker and was the winner of the second largest live field tournament in Ireland - a Party Poker Dublin tournament with well over 2000 players.

What happened in poker when the solvers took over?

The average standard got higher. A large percentage of the perceived top poker players these days "learn" what their predecessors did using the trial and error, empirical approach. Note the word "perceived". The specific solver inputs must come from somewhere - so who helps program them?

Millions of hands were played by the best guys like me in the previous era to narrow down bet sizing, ranges, frequencies etc. The difference nowadays is that the top poker players studying the solvers might be able to do what we did with all this information given to them, but maybe they won't understand why a particular play is best in a spot. How useful is that? It's very limited. The very top poker players will still have the probabilistic aptitude and ability to deviate from *theoretical* optimal game play for every different situation. This will never change.

Any top old school player who has now implemented solver study (when needed) into their play will be dangerous at the tables. It's the very same in sports betting - a small percentage of sports bettors will be proper handicappers and watchers of the sports they bet. They may also have adapted to building or using a strong blend of quantitative, qualitative or Bayesian sports betting models. It's very rare you'll find someone highly skilled in all areas which is why networking is also important in this day and age. The likes of Billy Walters had a big team behind him in covering all departments. From a sportsbook point of view, the sharp bookmakers like Pinnacle will use this concept. Without a lot of experience actually watching the sports, monitoring the markets and making bets, the predominantly maths-based sports bettors often think they can use advanced maths expertise and back testing by applying it to big sample data, and then use their findings to beat the markets. This is largely futile for most.

It's very similar to the highly mathematical orientated poker players immersing themselves in solver study and thinking they can beat the guys who did it all empirically. Both predominantly maths-based approaches are limited and put the handcuffs on. Without experience in the markets, how do you quantify results and weigh performance? Not to mention the fact you are using similar data to where the odds came from, and those odds also have a margin built in.

"There's a big difference between being a maths expert and an expert sports bettor"

I'm an empirical learner. I learned everything I know through trial and error, documenting and recording results and seeing patterns. People like Phil Galfond and Doug Polk are the same, albeit Polk uses the solvers too. He mentions that it feels like it's a battle of the logical mathematicians and the frequentists:

Doug Polk: "*I feel like it kind of killed the soul of the game, changing poker from who can be the most creative problem-solver to who can memorise the most stuff and apply it*"

Theoretically this is the same maths wise as sports betting. A lot of assumptions are made and when you look at each hand individually (like markets and bets individually) you see you can exploit it. It's exactly the same now with the models coming in and the noise alongside them. The models in sports betting are the solvers in poker and guys who are maybe good at maths but don't really understand the markets / sports (similar to not knowing why they are making certain poker plays the solvers says) means they are very exploitable. The reality is most of them talk a good game but are around break even. Not too strange though, right? As equilibrium is actually their game. Essentially, they are standing outside the "black box" and making assumptions. They are seeing the long-term average outputs as correct, whereas I'm inside the black box manning the controls and can see that a lot of what they are saying is rubbish.

How can you exploit tendencies and situations if you can't see them?

These guys are on the outside looking in. Again, there's a big difference in being a maths or analytics expert to being a sports betting expert or even a top-class poker player. You are very limited as one of these guys and beating the rake / margin is extremely hard in this regard. They can't factor in enough qualitative or subjective stuff that isn't in the price as they don't know what the stuff is they are looking for and can't quantify it.

Game Theory Optimal (GTO)

Game theory optimal is a mathematical concept whereby if you play it you can't be exploited. Two people employing this style will be in a state of equilibrium. It's about making the most +EV decisions given your opponents presumed optimal style.

There were a small percentage of players who by trial and error figured out all the right bet sizings and ranges before the push fold charts etc came out. We did it empirically.

The reality is that in real time no human can employ Game Theory Optimal perfectly without real time assistance (RTAs). Playing this style, you won't make the most money you can vs certain types of opponents, where an exploitative style would return the most positive expected value.

On average you can't be exploited but that's not to say certain people can't take advantage of you. You're exploiting yourself in a way by leaving money on the table.

Rock, Paper, Scissors Theory

If you play Rock, Scissors, Paper picking each one 33% of the time against an opponent who is randomly doing the same, you break even in the end. Or do you? What if you picked up a pattern in your opponent's "random" selections?

For example: every fifth pick was always Rock. You'd now have big positive expectation against this particular opponent and it's the same in poker...

Consider this: your bluff frequency on certain boards on the river is 30%. A certain opponent knows this. Said opponent has also picked up a tell where your nose twitches the 30% of times you are bluffing and it doesn't the 70% of time you are value betting. This opponent has huge EV against you by always correctly folding and calling your river bets.

GTO means you theoretically can't be exploited over the long term but what happens is you actually exploit yourself by not deviating from this strategy (see example above). You don't win the max and lose the least in each situation taken in a vacuum. Conditional probability applied to each different situation is the most truly optimal way to play. Poker is all about probabilities and implied odds but in terms of gaining an edge it's mainly about conditional probability changing the odds and taking advantage of this in the numbers.

The biggest tourney score for me was in an event where I nearly didn't play. I own this tourney due to the structure and the fact it was in my wheelhouse coinciding with my background playing STTs as my forte. Most people were making the same mistakes such as opening too wide from bad positions with marginal hands.

This is a common fundamental mistake most poker players make in all game types by the way but particularly in this type of structure where a lot of stacks were around the 20bb mark. It led to big errors, getting pot committed with bad hands. People didn't adjust for the different variables and specific game dynamics, and this concept transfers to sports betting markets.

For me this is the best version of this pic - you may have seen it around the internet

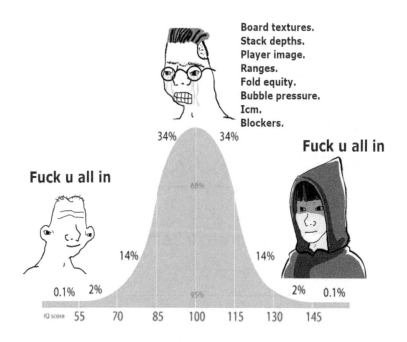

What this means is basically that the best players can automatically do through empirical evidence and intuition what the people of average to limited intellect are doing with their studying. The average ones are the ones you'll hear around the internet with their solver and technical talk and they'll usually, but not always, be very limited players despite the way they speak. This analogy applies with sports betting and the academics and maths guys - they'll often be the guys in the middle working hard, possibly to little avail. Many traders for the firms will also be in this category.

If these guys are winning it's often largely due to discipline and a strict mathematical approach, not high skill levels. They may learn things off by heart and don't understand what's behind them - exactly like the guys who think betting markets are efficient without being able to dissect them and really understand them. Both the bad player and the smart player above are thinking the same thing, but for different reasons. The bad player just wants to see the cards and show down, the good player knows he must fold.

To make money, invest with odds overwhelmingly in your favour -

Lauren Roberts

Game selection in Sports Betting, Poker and Daily Fantasy Sports

In poker you're only as good as the players you're playing against. If you're the sixth best player in the country but you always sit in a cash game with the five best players, you're going to lose long term. Game selection is huge in whatever form of gambling you are partaking in. In DFS if you play in large field, multiple entry tournaments you're reducing any skill edge you may have purely by default. This is because daily fantasy sports is about combinations and permutations. The more entries there are - especially if there are skilled players with hundreds of line-ups in the GPPs - the more combinations that are covered.

As an example, we can take the milli-maker in daily fantasy golf on DraftKings in the largest GPP (guaranteed prize pool) field of the week where we usually win 100k to 200k for top prize in a run of the mill event. Cost of entry is usually $15 - 20$ only per team. Most people think this is great value. It is not. The big money is right up the top and the prize structure is poor. We literally have to have one of our team entries of six players finish something like 1st, 3rd, 4th, 8th, 10th and 16th to have a chance to win or claim one of the big money prizes.

Do you know how hard that is to do in golf despite your knowledge and skills predicting course fit and other areas? Yes, too hard. It's extremely unlikely to even have six from six make the cut. You're playing the DFS golf lotto and even if you are super skilled at narrowing down the fields and putting together plus EV line ups, you're still playing with little to no edge given the rake taken. A +EV skill edge you have can only be pushed by playing smart. Target smaller fields, better payout structures, capped entry, or single entry only events. It's a lot easier to rise through the stakes playing this way too as there's a much higher chance of a return and minimising variance.

If you're breaking even most weeks, what do the stakes matter, bigger buy ins then become just an investment. **This only applies to very skilled players**.

Poker works the same way. I used to target the $109 tournaments on Stars which had decent quality smaller fields and good payout structures. I found I could really push my skill edge in these tournaments and minimise variance at the same time.

It's the very same in sports betting. How do you exploit it? Stay away from the higher liquidity and more popular markets. They are the more efficient markets, generally speaking. No matter how skilled you are you can't beat an efficient market (accurately priced) in the long run, especially one with a margin built in. Prop markets and large multi-field markets are good to try and find an edge in. Some sports are better than others to bet.

Look for markets with higher overround: a common misconception is these are hard to beat, but they have that overround implemented because of uncertainty in the price.

Restrictions, profiling and factoring - What is stake factoring?

Otherwise known as limiting or restrictions, I'll explain exactly what happens here. It's all about monitoring player behaviour and betting patterns. Betting companies have things automated so that they are on the lookout to track and flag potential profitable customers. A couple of the biggest things tracked are if customers use odds comparison services, and if they beat the closing price regularly.

- What site did you come from?
- Did you take the top price?
- What sort of staking are they using?
- What markets are they betting into and when?
- Are you following tipsters?
- Are you beating the closing line?

There are many more criteria being profiled by a specific department and you might be surprised by the data the bookmakers have on you. Different companies can and do share this info. Some guys have access to multiple accounts of yours, maybe even guys you know from Twitter can see your Profit & Loss and betting behaviour!

Stake factoring and limits

When you open new accounts, they are just normal and have what is called a stake factor of 1 applied. This means you can bet to win whatever the limits are in the particular market at the time of your bet. Your stake factor can be adjusted as time goes on and more data about your betting patterns and tendencies is collected. As markets become more mature the automatic limits go up. This will influence how much you can bet. Generally speaking, limits will be lower for everyone closer to the market openers.

If you have a stake factor of 0.5, for example, then whatever the liability limit is on the market you're betting at the time, you personally can only bet to win half this amount. 0.1 = 1/10 of this limit. Stake factors can range from less than 0.1 up to around 5 for VIP accounts. VIP accounts are basically high staking whales the bookmakers prey on with extra perks etc. It's bad practice.

Stake factoring and profiling is about the algorithm monitoring your movements and patterns, but traders can also have a say on certain accounts: I once got a 'to make the cut multiple' in with one firm and the next week multiples were taken away from me in this market. Like most things in sports betting, each individual situation is different. The main golf trader at said firm actually commented specifically on the tweet I made detailing the bet. The bet came in quite easily and the following week I was restricted to doubles for a time - no bigger multiples on cut bets.

Some bettors will be factored and limited, some won't, and vice versa. Some are banned from other markets and handcuffed as to what bets they can make. You might be restricted at some bookmakers and have bad things to say about them and only good things to say about another, only for someone else to be the opposite.

Restrictions inevitably come into place for me, and I get severely factored in markets I do well in. You might receive an email telling you that you can't bet in certain subsidiary markets (they call them novelty markets) or you can't take advantage of particular special offers or perks. Some books like to ask for "documents" over and over.

Take anyone on social media with a pinch of salt if they are on there boasting about account restrictions and stake factoring because that's all they are doing, however they dress it up. It's not as bad as is usually made out. Not if you are a twenty to one hundred quid bettor let's say. The above example is common practice these days. Documents you've posted before will be re-requested and hoops will have to be jumped. This will rarely happen if you are losing or engaging in fish like betting practices.

Affordability checks are the new thing and they are a real danger to sports betting. Imagine a bunch of strangers requesting your bank statements in any walk of life, never mind your bookmaker(s). Who in their right mind would be happy to give this personal information out?

Can we lift the limits? Yes.

I played bingo and dodgy - EV submarkets during covid. I was bored. Coincidentally, the result was two bookmakers easing my restrictions for a period. There are things you can do to make your account look very "recreational" and this is a part of the new era for serious sports bettors as they look to get more "outs".

Having none of it

I suppose the best example I can give through personal experience of what can happen regarding restrictions with corporate bookmakers if you are a shrewd sports bettor is to recall a time when I opened an account to take advantage of generous each way terms in golf. It was ahead of the PGA championship that Justin Thomas won at Quail Hollow.

At the time the firm in question was offering 1/5th ten places and this was in the very early days of this type of promotional market product offering. Prices were competitive as well with the general odds being around 85-90% of the average across the board. Thomas was 40/1 as compared to top price on the Oddschecker grid of 50s.

I lodged a grand and spread it across seven or eight golfers each way. Thomas was the biggest bet at €100 EW. He won. I staked in such a way that I was next to freerolling given my golf betting knowledge of the players and Quail Hollow specifically. To cut a long story short, that was my first week with the bookmaker and I had a 400% return on investment. The following week I was restricted to pennies in all markets, rendering the account done and dusted. I was made to jump through hoops to get my withdrawal.

How do we beat the betting markets? A Summary

The following chapter is a synopsis of how we can beat the markets going forward. I say I don't give too much stuff away that I really shouldn't. I lied. This is arguably the most important few chapters of the book and of your betting journey.

"Know your enemy to beat your enemy"

Exploit the markets using conditional probability. First thing's first: You are not betting against some future predicting geniuses. When I talk to my friends who bet recreationally most of them seem to have this predisposition that whoever is setting the lines and sitting on the other side of the fence is running some sort of supercomputer operation. They are not.

If you look at the job pages on many sports betting company websites now, you'll see the skills needed are mainly strong numerical ability and fluency in excel. Some sites even say sports and betting knowledge is not essential, which is mad right? Not really. In house odds are automated by data feeds and models. Traders "add value" by monitoring and moving lines in accordance with the market, and they add margins in relation to their clients. VIP players are looked after. The lines are dictated by consultancy companies or the exchange for the most part.

Regardless of the margins, you might think it's hard not to be able to find some angles to beat markets that are automated in this way - markets that might be monitored by people that quite literally don't have a clue and are advertised as such. You'd be right. The real problem pro and serious bettors have is not beating the market (and margins), it's getting enough money down to make it worthwhile.

Shrewdies accounts are factored / limited, and this process added to the protection and commission margin barrier is how bookies win overall. Bookmakers have an edge over the crowd mainly due to the margin they build into their odds and books. This is known as the overround and it's what produces their commission which is known as the juice or the vigorish. It's used to protect them against uncertainty and bigger players.
Many average bettors would be able to beat the bookmaker prices if it wasn't for that margin. Remember this fact.

For example:

If a race has five horses of the same ability and all variables are the same in theory, then all horses should be 4/1 to win, which represents a 20% chance for each of five. The bookmaker might price these horses at 3/1 which would equate to 25%-win probability. This is a bit of an exaggeration - they are not that greedy but just to keep it simple. The five horses together would now equal a 125% overround book - this extra 25% is known as the overround or combined margin (the "hold" in US betting terminology).

Let's say the traders took 100$ on each horse. Their handle / turnover would be 500$. Whatever horse wins they would only pay out 400$. They have now made a profit of 20% on their turnover which is their commission (vig or juice). Note how (written as a percentage) the commission figure differs from the 25% overround / margin number.

Market Efficiency - how beatable are the Odds?

I'll make a strong case for the supposedly efficient markets (high liquidity markets) not even being as efficient as is believed, but for now I'll just take you through how and why markets are beatable. First of all, they are not as soft as they used to be but there are many opportunities if you are selective. This is key to beating the game these days. I'd argue a case for you to diversify and spend time researching other players and who can beat other sports and get them onside to diversify your portfolio: this can be a big part of profitability nowadays. Being a judge of judges. Markets are based on what's known as BIG DATA. Usually large sample sizes of statistics, and averages. Gaussian distributions with constant / linear deviations.

Averages are rubbish. Small data and conditional probability are what rules in sports when we want actual true probabilities for each runner. Small sample sizes have more predictability than you would imagine if you know what you are looking for. The market must be set this way to cater for all monies incoming and to save resources. It works, but largely due to factoring and restricting of the sharp players. Traders in house can move their lines. Therefore, we can all win. This is how we can beat the markets.

Imagine fifty coin flips coming up thirty heads and twenty tails and then pricing up 4/6 and 6/4 due to this - we often see this kind of thing in the pricing of markets, especially props. Does it mean the probability of tails on the next flip is 40%? No, it does not. It's still 50% which equates to odds of even money, so if you keep taking the value on the 6/4 over a theoretically high volume of value bets you will make some nice money over time. Props are priced over small samples of data as if they are uniform probabilities like a coin flip. They are way different in reality.

Some facts about going Pro

Although it's getting harder to make money sports betting, the facts are if you bet odds continuously with the percentage edge in your favour you will win over time, when variance evens out. This can take quite a while so patience is important. Diversification, hedging and strong risk and bankroll management are all key to the process. As is Line Shopping. The markets will offer up plenty of opportunity to bet with the edge in your favour, you need to wait and be selective. Selectivity is key.

If you make consistent positive expectation (+ EV) bets you will win long term.

Positive expected value bets are there, and they are bettable, you just need to be patient and pick off the best opportunities. This requires a bit of work and shopping around, even if it means going to offshore books or around the physical location shops. You will have to work very hard if you want to be professional. Accounts are a problem, and you will need avenues to open as many as you can. Networking is a lot easier these days. If you stake large enough this will equate to an income. A solid staking plan is needed to withstand variance and keep you in the game.

How do I learn to bet smarter?

- Work on your discipline
- Look into networking
- Think about scaling up
- Listen to betting podcasts
- Absorb educational betting content
- Game selection most important aspect?
- Learn about bankroll management and risk
- Proper staking strategy
- Reduce variance by targeting lower odds markets
- Bet Props and derivative markets
- Line shop and have multiple accounts
- Discords and slack communities
- Use brokers and PPH accounts
- Take advantage of sign up offers, promos and bonuses

Data science and analytics is becoming the way forward in all working sectors. Modelling and algorithms are going to become common practice whether we like it or not. There are options to learn about different areas of data science online using Data Camps and websites offering courses and tutorials from home without signing up for anything official and maybe paying substantial money. You can take proper accredited courses as well.

When I was young, I wished there were some sort of sports betting courses available. I would have preferred a curriculum in a physical college or location with a qualification at the end of it. There are now some online courses available in this area with the likes of Zoom, Slack and various softwares making it possible. These courses won't be cheap if you sign up for genuine quality but are an area worth considering.

There are several educational and sports betting resources sites available, as well as betting sites offering software and tools for aid. There's value betting software available that tracks sharp vs soft bookmakers' prices and flags up value re price movements. My own site Sharp Sports Bettors is the best place to go to get access to all these resources and high-level content from various experts in the industry.

Make sure to check that out and buy Angles & Edges and Book no. 3 of the trilogy, coming soon.

Bryan Nicholson is a sports betting handicapper, analyst and +EV sports bettor and poker player with a long-time edge in the betting industry, applying probability skills he learned in college through Engineering, along with logic to beating the betting markets. He has worked with and consulted with several betting firms and syndicate players. Author of specialist golf betting book "Angles & Edges", he ran one of the most profitable long term online betting services of all time.

HYPNOTISED BY NUMBERS REVIEW

Guys, I hope you enjoyed my second book on sports betting and there's more to come in book number three. If you read and enjoyed *Hypnotised By Numbers*, I would be grateful if you'd take a minute to go to the amazon or specific marketplace page you bought it from and leave a short review and or rating. If you would spread the word about the book on your social media that would be great as well! Thanks for reading and all the best.

Bryan

Printed in Great Britain
by Amazon

43390151R00096